NEW COLLEGE
LECTURES

WRITING IN RIGHTS

AUSTRALIA AND THE PROTECTION OF HUMAN RIGHTS

Hilary Charlesworth

**UNSW
PRESS**

A UNSW Press book

Published by
University of New South Wales Press Ltd
University of New South Wales
UNSW Sydney NSW 2052
AUSTRALIA
www.unswpress.com.au

© The Trustees of the New College Lectures 2002
First published 2002

National Library of Australia
Cataloguing-in-Publication entry:

Charlesworth, H.C. (Hilary C.).
Writing in rights: Australia and the protection of human rights.

ISBN 0 86840 788 7.

1. Human rights — Australia. 2. Civil rights — Australia.
I. Title. (Series: New College lectures).

323.0994

Printer Ligare

NEW COLLEGE
LECTURES
AND
PUBLICATIONS

New College is an Anglican college affiliated with the University of New South Wales, Sydney. In 1986 the college set up a trust to conduct an annual series of public lectures. The lecturer is asked to take up some aspect of contemporary society and to comment on it from the standpoint of their Christian faith and professional experience. The inaugural lectures were given in 1987 by Professor Malcolm Jeeves of the University of St Andrews, Scotland, and in subsequent years lecturers have come from Australian and overseas universities, as well as the wider community.

1987   Prof Malcolm Jeeves (University of St Andrews, Scotland)
        Minefields, Lancer Books (ANZEA), 1994.
1988   Veronica Brady (University of Western Australia)
        Can These Bones Live? Federation Press, 1997.
1989   The Hon Keith Justice Mason (NSW Supreme Court)
        Constancy and Change, Federation Press, 1990.
1990   Prof Stanley Hauerwas (Duke University, USA)
        After Christendom? ANZEA, 1991.
1991   Prof Geoffrey Bolton (University of Queensland).
1992   Prof Peter Newman (Murdoch University, Western Australia).
1993   Prof Robin Gill (University of Kent, England)
        Beyond Self Interest, New College, 1993.
        Rev Dr John Polkinghorne, KBE, FRS (Queens' College, Cambridge, England)
        Religion and Current Science, New College, 1993.
1994   Prof Geoffrey Brennan (Australian National University).
1995   Rev Dr John Polkinghorne, KBE, FRS (Queens' College, Cambridge, England)
        Beyond Science, Cambridge University Press, 1996; Polish ed, 1998; Greek ed, 1999.

1996   Les Murray (Australian poet)
Killing the Black Dog, Federation Press, 1997.

1997   Dr Elaine Storkey (London Institute for Contemporary Christianity, England)
Created or Constructed? The Great Gender Debate, Paternoster Press, 2000; UNSW Press, 2001.

1998   Dr Peter Vardy (Heythrop College, University of London, England)
What is Truth? UNSW Press, 1999.

1999   Prof William J Baker (University of Maine, USA)
If Christ Came to the Olympics, UNSW Press, 2000.

2000   Prof Hilary Charlesworth (Australian National University, Canberra)
Writing in Rights, UNSW Press, 2002.

CONTENTS

Foreword by Allan Beavis   9

Introduction   13

1   A constitutional silence   17

2   The international human rights system   41

3   Protecting human rights in Australia   56

Appendix A   78
The Australian Constitution 1901 (extracts)

Appendix B   79
Canadian Charter of Rights and Freedoms 1982

Appendix C   84
South African Constitution 1996 (Bill of Rights)

Appendix D   96
United Kingdom Human Rights Act 1998

Notes   104

FOREWORD

by Allan Beavis
Master, New College UNSW

RETHINKING OUR CONSTITUTION: HUMAN RIGHTS PERSPECTIVES

One of the goals of the annual New College Lectures is to provide an opportunity for a distinguished scholar to comment upon some aspect of contemporary life and society consistent with the objects and purposes of New College. The 2000 Lectures were delivered in the year leading up to the centenary of two important milestones in the life of Australian society — federation and the Australian Constitution. The Lectures Trustees decided to celebrate the occasion by inviting someone to reflect upon the Australian Constitution in the light of contemporary society's concern for human rights, thus contributing to the debate concerning constitutional change that has been in progress for several years. Following much consideration, Hilary Charlesworth, Professor and Director of the Centre for International and Public Law at the Australian National University, was invited to deliver a set of three lectures on this topic. Her research and teaching in international law and human rights law have won her international acclaim, and her ability to address issues as a Christian has been amply demonstrated in public fora.

The topic of human rights is central in legal and political discourse in contemporary Australia, as well as being a topic that ought to be of vital interest to those of Christian belief and commitment. There is a strong case to be made that human rights find their origins in religion, be it Jewish, Christian, Muslim, Hindu or Buddhist. On the other hand, there is an equally strong case that suggests it is far too early to speak of any 'Christian tradition' of human rights. Evangelical Christians, in particular, have often emphasised duties rather than rights, arguing that the Bible does not provide justification for the proposition that human beings have inherent or *a priori* rights simply on the basis of existence. Rather, the Bible appears to support divinely imposed duties, and what we currently call human rights are the contingent concomitants of those duties. Catholic Christians have also emphasised the 'Rights of God' over the 'Rights of Man'. Some even argue that the 'religion' that has given impetus to human rights is the 'secularism' based upon a global consensus that embraces both humanists and the world's great religions. Although the relationship between religion and human rights is unresolved, Christians nevertheless have a unique opportunity to contribute to the ongoing discussion of human rights in contemporary society.

A number of factors suggest that this discussion will take on greater urgency in Australian society as we move into the 21st century. For one thing, there is pressure from some sections of the community for an Australian bill of rights to be incorporated into our legal system. This is given impetus by the ever-increasing intrusion of the state into the daily lives of individuals, as well as the difficult issue of its relationship with indigenous people. Then there is the burgeoning of centres for the study of human rights in the tertiary sector. The trickle-down effect of this research and scholarship will inevitably impact on the wider social scene. It is therefore timely to have Hilary Charlesworth's careful analysis of the role of the Australian Constitution in relation to human rights; her clear overview of the development of the international human rights movement; and her perceptive views on possible future relationships between the Australian Constitution and the protection of human rights. And given the historical ambiguities inherent in the relationship between Christianity and human rights at both the Catholic and Evangelical ends of the spectrum, this book offers conceptual clarification that can only be helpful to the contributions that individual Christians and the Christian community at large can make to this debate.

The New College Lectures have a proud history and the list of previous lecturers and publications is impressive. The Lectures are delivered within the academic context of the University of New South Wales, and the lecturers are given freedom to handle the agreed topic as they choose. The views they express are not necessarily those of the College.

The Trustees thank Hilary Charlesworth for a splendid series of lectures and a publication that enhances the contribution of this series to Australian society. They are also grateful to Robin Derricourt and Nicola Young from UNSW Press for their assistance in publication.

INTRODUCTION

A centenary is an arbitrary chronological division. It is also, as Frank Kermode has pointed out, a milestone that provides an end of which everyone is aware and 'in which we take a complex comfort'. It allows us to 'project our existential anxieties on to history'.[1] The idea of the centenary of Australia's federation provides the chance to take stock and to imagine that the future can somehow be brighter and better than the past.

The celebrations in 2001 of the centenary of Australia's federation have generally been proud, indeed almost triumphal. Accounts of the rocky history of the federation movement and the lives and hopes of the men (and occasional woman) who participated in it have dominated the public festivities. The primary document of federation, the Australian Constitution, has also been in the spotlight along with its drafters, their characters, debates, quarrels and compromises. The stability promoted by the Constitution has been admired, as has the document's capacity to adapt to changing conditions. There has been renewed attention to the development of the major institutions of Australian public life and the creation of an Australian ethos and sensibility.

The long-term value of these celebrations will be reduced, however, if we ignore those areas where we have made little progress over the last 100 years and fail to plan for change. This book examines one aspect of

Australian political and legal life where time seems to have stood almost still over the last century: the protection of human rights. The architects of federation considered an inclusion of some forms of human rights protection in the Constitution, but eventually decided that they would too greatly disturb the fabric of colonial society. Politicians today echo these fears, arguing both that Australia is a world leader in upholding its population's human rights and that establishing a general system to redress breaches of human rights would undermine Australian democracy.

In this book, I try to show why these arguments are flawed and inadequate for our future. Chapter 1 considers the federation debate about rights and how subsequent Australian law has responded to the meagre constitutional directions about rights. Chapter 2 turns to an alternative source of human rights norms, the international legal system. This chapter also considers various objections to human rights principles from cultural, philosophical and religious perspectives. Chapter 3 suggests that the great Australian silence about human rights can be overcome to some extent by linking Australian law more clearly to international standards. This final chapter considers the lessons of three modern constitutional experiments with rights protection: Canada, South Africa and the United Kingdom.

Australia is now the only country in the common law world without a system for protecting human rights. My overall contention is that the second century of federation would be greatly enriched by the development of an Australian system for the protection of human rights. We should celebrate the centenary of federation by renewing and reinvigorating the debate about introducing guarantees of rights into our legal system.

The ideas in this book were presented as the New College Lectures in October 2000. I am very grateful to the Trustees of the New College Lectures for their invitation to give the lectures and particularly the Master of New College, Dr Allan Beavis, for his interest in their development and for his many acts of kindness. I am also in the debt of Ian Walker, the Acting Master at the time the lectures were delivered, for his warm hospitality and courtesy. I was most engaged by the commitment to public and community service of the New College students I met and through them grew in confidence about Australia's capacity to develop and change.

My colleagues Robert McCorquodale and Adrienne Stone generously helped me with information and ideas and Jillian Caldwell assisted greatly in polishing the footnotes. Charles Guest kept our home fires burning while I gave the lectures and he has talked over the themes contained in them for a long time. My wonderful father, Max Charlesworth, kindly corrected the proofs. I am also grateful to UNSW Press for its considerable assistance in publishing the lectures and to Claire de Medici for her excellent editorial eye.

I

A CONSTITUTIONAL SILENCE

RIGHTS IN THE AUSTRALIAN CONSTITUTION

Many Australians would be surprised, perhaps even shocked, that the Constitution — the foundational text of Australian public life — contains little mention of the relationship of governments to the people. Indeed, although the Constitution's preamble refers to the agreement of the people of the Australian colonies to federate, there are few further references to the Australian people in the document. The Constitution was, in essence, a compact first between a new country and its imperial parent and second between the former Australian colonies and a new federal government. The Constitution's focus is on the relationships between these old and new institutions. It seems, for example, much more concerned about preserving the freedom of interstate trade than creating the conditions for Australia's inhabitants to live rewarding lives. Overall, our Constitution is rather drab, overlaid with an anxiety about the preservation of a balance of power between the States and the Commonwealth in quite mechanical terms.

If we look closely at the document, we can find some traces of the idea that the power of governments over their population has limits. For example: the Commonwealth cannot prevent a person who has a right to vote in State elections from voting in federal elections (section 41); Commonwealth acquisition of property must be on just terms (section 51 (xxxi)); the

Commonwealth cannot conscript people to provide medical services (section 51 (xxxiiiA)). The establishment of a federal judicial system in Chapter III of the Constitution can be seen as a commitment to the rule of law, preventing the executive branch of government from acting outside the law.[1] But these traces add up to a rather limited account of the relationship between government and the people.

The Constitution contains three explicit references to the rights of people, but the language is hedged and technical. Section 80 sets out a citizen's right to a jury trial within the State where an offence took place, when charged on indictment for an offence under Commonwealth law; section 116 denies the Commonwealth Parliament (but not State Parliaments) the power to legislate to establish a religion, or to impose any religious observance, or to prohibit the free exercise of any religion, or to require a religious test as a qualification for public office; and section 117 protects residents of one State from discrimination by another State on the basis of residence. The Constitution says nothing at all about our rights to freedom of expression, to privacy, to health or education, or to any of the basic conditions of a life worth living.

THE INFLUENCE OF THE US MODEL

The overall silence about rights is surprising from a historical perspective. We know that the Australian constitutional drafters were very interested in the US Constitution as a model and were influenced by it in many respects. The US Constitution was the only example of a federal constitution in existence when talk of federation had begun in Australia in the 1840s, and by the time discussion of federation became serious, the US example was over 100 years old.

Late in the 19th century, there were also the Swiss (1848) and Canadian (1874) Constitutions to consider, but the US model appealed particularly to the Australian imagination because that model's structure coincided with the terms upon which the Australian colonies were prepared to federate. Shortly after the Australian Constitution was enacted in 1900, Inglis Clark, the Tasmanian lawyer who was one of its most influential drafters, said:

> [Our Constitution] so closely resembles the Constitution of the United States of America that it may not be improperly described as an adaptation of that Constitution to the political circumstances [of

the Australian colonies] ... and the authors of the American proto-
type may be fitly regarded as being also the primary authors of the
Constitution of the Commonwealth of Australia.[2]

This is a rather wishful description of the relationship between the two
Constitutions, undoubtedly due to Clark's great admiration for the US
Constitution and his constant advocacy during the 1890s of its relevance
as a model for Australia. However, many aspects of the Australian
Constitution were derived from the US model: for example, the provisions relating to the Senate and those establishing the Commonwealth
judicial system. The US Constitution also influenced the Australian
scheme of allocation of legislative powers between federal and State governments.

The US Constitution contains a long catalogue of rights in the Bill of
Rights, inserted in the Constitution in 1789, and in later amendments.
Indeed, most Americans identify their Constitution entirely with its statement of rights. American constitutional lawyers typically regard the creation and protection of individual rights as 'the highest function of any
government'.[3] Why then does the Australian Constitution contain only
fleeting, minimal, references to rights?

An explanation traditionally offered for the absence of a coherent bill
of rights in the Australian Constitution is a historical one. The years of tur-
moil in the United States that preceded the drafting and adoption of the
US Constitution's Bill of Rights and later constitutional amendments protecting individual liberties are given as the reason for the presence of these
guarantees. Because the Australian transition to federation was peaceful,
the argument goes, there was no need for the constitutional entrenchment
of individual rights.[4] Thus Justice Moffatt wrote:

> The Australians had no recent memory of a bitter struggle against
> tyranical devices to make them determine to erect permanent pro-
> tections against their use again ... [T]hey must have felt that the pro-
> tections to individual rights provided by the traditions of acting as
> honourable men were quite sufficient for a civilised society.[5]

Indeed, James Bryce, whose book *The American Commonwealth* greatly
influenced the Australian constitutional drafters, later described the
absence of constitutional protection of individual rights in the Australian
Constitution as proof of its modernity and its truly democratic character.[6]

THE RIGHTS DEBATE IN THE CONSTITUTIONAL CONVENTIONS

The Australian Constitution was drafted in two Conventions in the 1890s.[7] Almost all the initiatives with respect to rights were taken by Inglis Clark. Clark was the Tasmanian Attorney-General during much of this time and was a respected and active figure. He prepared a preliminary draft of a constitution in 1890, which deeply influenced the first official draft produced by Queensland Premier Samuel Griffith in 1891. Clark had travelled in the United States and maintained an energetic correspondence with one of the grand figures of American law, Oliver Wendell Holmes. Clark was an enthusiast for the United States — 'a country to which in spirit he belonged, whose Constitution he reverenced, and whose great men he idolised', as Alfred Deakin said of him.[8] Clark articulated a rationale for the inclusion of individual rights in a constitution. He wrote of:

> The essentially republican doctrine of the natural, or ... the rational rights of man ... [that] may be ... ultimately found to be the true and final justification of all resistance to the tyranny of the majority, whose unrestricted rule is so often and so erroneously regarded as the essence and distinctive principle of democracy. The unrestricted use of the majority of the hour is at all times a contradiction of the rational rights of the individual.[9]

Clark's draft did not reproduce the entire catalogue of rights found in the US Constitution, but featured just four: the right to a jury trial, to the privileges and immunities of State citizenship, to equal protection under the law and due process, and to freedom of and non-establishment of religion. Why was Clark so modest in his borrowing from the US Constitution? Why, for example, did he seek to protect religion and not other rights contained in the US Constitution's First Amendment, such as freedom of speech and press, of peaceful assembly and petition for grievances? Why did he borrow a limited right to jury trial and not the broader protection afforded by the Sixth and Eighth Amendments that insist on speedy and public trials, jury trials in all criminal prosecutions, the assistance of counsel for defence, and that prohibit excessive bails and fines as well as cruel and unjust punishments? Perhaps this was because many of the US constitutional rights had not been invoked by the 1890s and did not appear as central as they do today. The US Constitution's First Amendment's guarantee of freedom of expression, for example, had little prominence in constitutional debate until after the First World War.[10] The guarantee of free exercise of religion, by contrast, had been discussed at length by the US Supreme Court in 1878.[11] And the Fourteenth Amendment's provisions on privileges and immunities of citizenship had had a significant effect on US jurisprudence by the 1890s.[12]

In any event, Clark's bold inclusion of some rights in his draft constitution met with considerable resistance from his fellow drafters. Some parts ultimately survived in the shadowy and wan form that we find them today. For example, Clark's right to a jury trial for all indictable offences under Commonwealth law was whittled back to give the federal government considerable discretion to be able to avoid a jury trial through using a summary procedure rather than an indictment.

Clark had proposed rights — modelled on the First Amendment to the US Constitution — to the free exercise of religion that would bind both Commonwealth and State governments. In Clark's draft, the Commonwealth would also be prohibited from establishing any religion. The restraint on State legislative power with respect to religion was ultimately dropped during the convention debates because it was thought impossible that a State would ever prohibit the free exercise of religion and because the provision was regarded as an unwarranted restriction on State legislative power. In Melbourne in 1898 Edmund Barton argued that 'there was no likelihood of any state ever prohibiting the free exercise of any religion — that there had been nothing of this kind in the past, and that there was not the slightest reason to expect the occurrence of any such thing in the future'.[13] After much debate, the delegates agreed to restrict Commonwealth power with respect to religion, not so much to protect individual freedom of religion, but to preserve State legislative power in this area. 'There are a number of sects in different parts of the world whose religious observances embrace every form of horror one can imagine', warned John Alexander Cockburn. This, he believed, proved that '[t]he states should be allowed to retain the right to do what they think necessary to preserve and maintain their civilisation'.[14] Edmund Barton argued unsuccessfully that the same assumption should apply in the case of the Commonwealth government, which he believed would be less parochial and superior in character to the State governments.[15]

Clark endeavoured to insert the language of equal protection of the laws and due process into the Constitution as part of a privileges and

immunities clause based on the US Constitution. His attempts were an
abject failure. In 1897 Clark proposed a clause in these terms:

> The citizens of each State, and all other persons owing allegiance to
> the Queen and residing in any territory of the Commonwealth, shall
> be citizens of the Commonwealth, and shall be entitled to all the priv-
> ileges and immunities of the citizens of the Commonwealth in the
> several States, and a State shall not make or enforce any law abridg-
> ing any privilege or immunity of citizens of the Commonwealth, nor
> shall a State deprive any person of life, liberty or property without
> due process of law, or deny to any person, within its jurisdiction equal
> protection of its laws.[16]

Certain contradictory themes recur in the debates. The immediate charge
was that the provision was couched in general and uncertain language. This
criticism was typically followed by the objection that the provision would
have too certain an impact, because it could have the effect of invalidating
colonial legislation, particularly legislation that discriminated against non-
European workers. The US origin of the clause was regarded with suspicion. It was argued that the peculiarity of the historical situation that
produced the US provision in itself demonstrated that it was irrelevant for
Australian conditions. At the same time, judicial interpretation of the
clause in the US Constitution was sometimes relied upon to establish that
it could have far-reaching and unsettling implications for the legal order of
the Australian colonies.

Behind these arguments was a concern about preserving the greatest
possible sphere of State autonomy. Robert Garran's *Australian Handbook of
Federal Government*, published in 1897, foreshadowed the course of the
debate in the Convention. Garran argued that few of the US Constitution's
provisions relating to individual rights were relevant to Australia. They
were either trivial or already amply secured. He described the idea of a declaration of rights as 'an interference with state rights, on behalf of popular
rights: an interference undoubtedly justifiable, if necessary, but if not necessary, better dispensed with'.[17]

Sir John Forrest, then Premier of Western Australia, warned the
Melbourne Convention in 1898 that an equal protection clause would create particular difficulties with coloured residents of his State. Western
Australian legislation prevented Asian or African aliens from obtaining mining rights or privileges without permission of the government, and imposed

an absolute ban on the employment of Asians and Africans as miners. Forrest feared that if such aliens were resident in other parts of Australia and not subject to similar restrictions, they would be able to invoke the clause to avoid the Western Australian restrictions. He spoke frankly:

> It is of no use for us to shut our eyes to the fact that there is a great feeling all over Australia against the introduction of coloured persons. It goes without saying that we do not like to talk about it, but still it is so. I do not want this clause to pass in a shape which would undo what is about to be done in most of the colonies ... in regard to that class of persons. It seems to me that should the clause be passed in its present shape, if a person, whatever his nationality, his colour or his character may be, happens to live in one state, another state could not legislate in any way to prohibit his entrance into that state.[18]

Forrest conceded that the new Commonwealth Parliament would have the power to enact legislation that could override such State laws. He objected, however, to their automatic invalidation by a constitutional prohibition. Isaac Isaacs, later Chief Justice of the High Court and Governor-General, also warned of the dangers of the language of equal protection, and the possibility that a clause could invalidate State factory legislation that restricted the employment of Asian workers. He pointed to a US Supreme Court decision where a Chinese alien had successfully invoked the equal protection clause to strike down a local ordinance regulating laundries[19] as proof of this danger.[20]

John Alexander Cockburn, one-time Premier of South Australia, took a different tack to argue that Inglis Clark's clause had no place in an Australian Constitution. He pointed out that the Fourteenth Amendment on which the clause was based had not been included in the original US Constitution and, he said, had simply been introduced by the victorious North as a punishment for the Southern States. This led Cockburn to question the clause's constitutional status: 'I do not believe this amendment was ever legally carried', he announced. He continued:

> I believe it was only carried by force of arms, by placing the voting places practically under martial law ... We do not want to imitate that example. We do not want a clause in our Constitution which could only be carried in America by force of arms ... I do not think we should pay it the compliment of imitating it here.[21]

The final version of section 117 appeared thus:

> A subject of the Queen, resident in any State, shall not be subject in any other State to any disability or discrimination which would not be equally applicable to him if he were a subject of the Queen resident in such other State.

The convoluted wording of this final version is a result of the drafters' determination to preserve a State's right to distinguish on racial grounds between classes of persons coming within its jurisdiction. The clause was recast in the negative in order to narrow its scope. The aim was to prevent discrimination 'based upon a false principle'. The clause would not, it was explained, impinge upon Sir John Forrest's law that prevented Asians obtaining mining rights in Western Australia, because '[t]here is no discrimination there based on residence or citizenship; it is simply based upon colour and race'.[22]

By contrast, Richard O'Connor, the NSW Solicitor-General, argued for the inclusion of a due process clause in the Constitution, on the grounds that '[w]e are making a Constitution which is to endure, practically speaking, for all time'. He went on:

> In the ordinary course of things such a provision would be unnecessary; but we all know that laws are passed by majorities and that communities are liable to sudden and very often to unjust impulses.[23]

This understanding of the role of constitutional guarantees shared by O'Connor and Inglis Clark did not, however, imply criticism of any existing laws. Both supported the idea of a white Australia. In 1888 Inglis Clark had warned of an influx of Chinese immigrants to justify restrictive immigration laws. He predicted that large numbers of Chinese would create racial divisions that could lead to civil war.[24]

In any event, the constitutional framers generally did not accept the notion that political majorities could be prone to 'unjust impulses' and should be limited by statements of individual rights. Isaac Isaacs and Alexander Cockburn in particular spoke strongly against it. Inclusion of guarantees of rights, they argued, would be an admission of their necessity. They were appropriate, said Cockburn, only in the constitution of a 'savage race'. He stated:

> [T]he insertion of these words would be a reflection on our civilisation. People would say: 'Pretty things these states of Australia; they

have to be prevented by a provision in the Constitution from doing the grossest injustice'.[25]

As we shall see, this type of argument has been remarkably durable in Australian constitutional history.

The constitutional drafters regularly commented on the deep racial inequality in US society that justified equal protection and due process guarantees. The drafters could see no parallels in Australia. It was accepted that Aborigines were inferior because they were so different to Europeans, and in any event Aborigines were assumed to be a dying race. Discrimination against other racial groups was reasonable and necessary to ensure the economic and cultural dominance of the Europeans. For Richard O'Connor, for example, federation would allow all coloured races to face similar disabilities. Helen Irving has pointed to the role that anti-Chinese feeling played in the process of Australian nation-building. The identification of a common enemy was a useful strategy in uniting the colonies' disparate interests.[26] It was also directly at odds with any notion that all individuals are 'naturally' endowed with rights.

The Australian rejection of the US system of rights guarantees was based above all on a concern to preserve the autonomy of the States. Consent to federation, it was argued, should not have implications for the way that a State dealt with any individual within its jurisdiction. This view was supported by what now appear to be contradictory arguments: the constantly expressed confidence that the States were unlikely to abridge any individual freedoms; and consensus that the power to enact racially discriminatory legislation was part of the inherent sovereignty of the States. The apparent contradiction is explained by the fact that a century ago in Australia discrimination against non-Europeans was not regarded as a matter of rights or freedoms. Early on in our constitutional history, therefore, the notion of States' rights was closely linked with the right to discriminate against racial minorities.

ANALYSING THE PAST

How critical should we be of the drafters of the Australian Constitution for the very narrow approach they took to the idea of rights, particularly their concern to allow racial discrimination? In other contexts, such as the debate over the 'stolen generation' of Aboriginal children, there have been many who argue that it is inappropriate to judge the past using modern standards of morality. The High Court's present Chief Justice, Murray Gleeson, has cautioned against slipping into an assumption of moral superiority when considering the values of the Constitution's framers.[27] He has pointed to the great changes between their world and ours. However, it is worth remembering that the Australian concern in the 1880s and 1890s to preserve a white society did meet with some contemporary resistance. The British were particularly concerned with immigration policies based explicitly on colour. This concern was partly driven by the desire to maintain good political and commercial relations with China and partly by the sense of the impropriety of distinguishing between subjects of the British Empire on the basis of race.[28] The candid acknowledgment by the constitutional drafters of their desire to preserve discriminatory State legislation was not, then, a simple reflection of accepted social prejudices.

There are two main reasons to subject the constitutional framers' motives to scrutiny today. The first is that, in many ways, these motives have deeply affected later discussion about rights. There have been remarkably unswerving themes in the debates over the last century: the most consistent has been the claim that the introduction of guarantees of rights would undermine our federal system by impinging on States' rights. For example, in the national debate in 2000 over whether the Northern Territory and Western Australian mandatory sentencing laws were a breach of human rights, a constant argument from all sides of politics was that the Commonwealth government should not intervene to overturn State and Territory legislation. The Prime Minister, Mr Howard, said that such action, while theoretically possible, would 'knock the federal system out of balance'.[29]

A second reason why it is important to remember the complex tangle of original objections to the inclusion of protection for rights in our Constitution is shown through analysis of more modern debates about reform of the Constitution. There is a tendency in Australia to attribute extraordinary foresight and wisdom to constitutional drafters, and to argue that it is inappropriate to tinker with the brilliance of their architecture. This type of pride is also found in US accounts of the drafting of their Constitution: the drafters are revered to an extraordinary level and endowed with almost god-like qualities. A more prosaically expressed variation of this tendency is summed up in the phrase 'if it ain't broke don't fix it'. Such a response to constitutional reform was widespread during the 1999 campaign over the Republic referendum. These approaches endow the status quo with great power and authority and make talk of reform appear almost wanton and irresponsible. 'We don't want change just for change's sake' has been an effective, if hackneyed, political riposte to proposals for Australian constitutional reform.

Investigating the ideas and motives of the constitutional drafters 100 years on provides a counterweight to the assumption of constitutional perfection, or at least constitutional sufficiency. If the reasons for particular silences and gaps in the Constitution can be shown to be neither heroic nor admirable by today's standards, the sanctity of the constitutional text is weakened and debate about its future becomes possible. An understanding of the motives of the constitutional founding fathers allows us to peel away excessive nostalgia about their wisdom.

THE INTERPRETATION OF CONSTITUTIONAL RIGHTS SINCE FEDERATION

What impact have the three surviving references to rights in the Constitution had in Australian jurisprudence? Overall, the restricted language in the rights provisions has been further eroded by their interpretation in litigation before the Australian High Court.

In one respect, the section 80 right to a jury trial for Commonwealth offences charged on indictment has been understood broadly. It has been interpreted to require that there be a unanimous jury verdict of guilty for indictable offences against Commonwealth law, on the belief that unanimity was an essential aspect of trial by jury at the time section 80 was drafted.[30] However, the provision's overall force has been whittled away by decisions holding that there were no restraints on the Commonwealth government's discretion to make an offence triable summarily or on indictment.[31] This discretion allows the Commonwealth government to avoid the need for a jury trial by defining an offence as summary. In 1965 Chief Justice Barwick spoke of this reading of section 80 as irresistible: 'What might have been thought to be a great constitutional provision,' he noted with an air of surprise, 'has been discovered to be a mere procedural provision'.[32]

In 2000 the High Court handed down a judgment on the scope of section 80 that reaffirmed the Commonwealth's discretion to deem an offence indictable or not. The High Court pointed out in the case of *Cheng v The Queen* that section 80 does not give a right to trial by jury for all *serious*

offences, but simply for offences deemed indictable.[33] This effectively gives
the Commonwealth complete power to determine when a jury trial is held.
The Commonwealth pointed to statements made during the constitutional conventions of the 1890s to claim that the founding fathers intended
section 80 of the Constitution to be an insubstantial guarantee. The majority of the High Court was influenced by this evidence, although the full
record of the constitutional debates reveals that the drafters' intentions may
well have been to limit the Commonwealth's discretion.[34]

In dissent, Justice Michael Kirby provided an alternative view of section 80 that would give it considerably more force. He criticised the 'ster-
ile' and 'withered' formalist view of the section approved by the majority of
the High Court. Justice Kirby said:

> [T]he framers of the Constitution did not intend, nor did they enjoy
> the power to require, that their subjective expectations, wishes or
> hopes should control all succeeding generations of Australians who
> live under the protection of the Constitution … [T]he consideration
> that governs the meaning of the constitutional text is the ascertain-
> ment, with the eyes of the present generation, of the essential char-
> acteristics of the text read as a constitutional charter of government.
> We are not chained to the expectations of 1900.[35]

This approach to constitutional interpretation of rights guarantees remains
a marginal perspective on the High Court.

Section 116 of the Australian Constitution — the prohibition on federal laws establishing or restricting the free exercise of religion — has had
very limited impact compared with its US ancestor, the First Amendment.
Section 116 has never been successfully invoked before the High Court
and has been interpreted in a very narrow manner, although in other contexts the Court has given the notion of 'religion' a very broad meaning.[36]
The High Court has held that, although the Commonwealth cannot
impose a national religion, it may assist the practice of religion by providing financial aid to religious schools without breaching the establishment
clause.[37] The majority of the High Court repudiated a view of section 116
as 'the repository of some broad statement of principle concerning the separation of church and state, from which may be distilled the detailed consequence of such separation'.[38] It was not a guarantee of a fundamental
human right, members of the majority said, but only a fetter on legislative
power of obscure origin. A narrow construction of the provision was

necessary because it was not part of a bill of rights and applied to the Commonwealth government alone.[39]

Three High Court cases in the last century raised the issue of whether Commonwealth laws restricted the free exercise of religion. *Krygger v Williams*[40] in 1912 involved a challenge to a law requiring all male residents to undergo military training, by a person whose religious beliefs forbad him to bear arms. Appeal to section 116 was given short shrift. Chief Justice Griffiths dismissed the claim of religious conscience as 'absurd'. He said '[t]o require a man to do a thing which has nothing at all to do with religion is not prohibiting him from a free exercise of religion'.[41] Justice Barton agreed: the objection to the military service legislation was 'as thin as anything of the kind that has come before us'.[42]

During the Second World War, the Jehovah's Witnesses challenged some national security regulations as, among other things, impeding the free exercise of religion, in violation of section 116 of the Constitution. The Jehovah's Witnesses advocated neutrality in wartime and refused to take an oath of allegiance to the King. The national security regulations, which were invoked against the group, prohibited the advocacy of doctrines prejudicial to the prosecution of the war. The regulations dissolved any association that engaged in this activity and vested its property in the Commonwealth. Chief Justice Latham, while describing the guarantee of religious tolerance in section 116 as 'overriding', insisted that it must be subordinate to laws, such as the national security regulations, that ensured the continued existence of society.[43] Although this may be an unsurprising decision in wartime, the Court took such a narrow view of the guarantee that it is unlikely that it would offer a protection of religious freedom even in times of peace. Justice Rich, for example, suggested that the dissolution of the Church's corporate structure had no effect on the free exercise of religion by its individual members.[44]

Section 116 was also raised in 1997 in *Kruger v Commonwealth*.[45] The plaintiffs argued that a Northern Territory ordinance that had authorised the removal of Aboriginal children from their families was constitutionally invalid because it effectively prohibited the free exercise of Aboriginal religion. The section 116 argument was rejected by the High Court on two grounds. It was unclear, first, whether section 116 affected the Commonwealth government's power to legislate with respect to Territories. Second, the Court found it difficult to find a breach of section 116's guarantee of free exercise of a religion because the terms of the ordinance required the Chief Protector of Aborigines to act on his opinion of the interests of the Aboriginal children. In the absence of other evidence, the words of the ordinance alone could not be construed as contrary to section 116. Only Justice Gaudron contemplated a broader scope for section 116. She favoured a 'liberal' construction of constitutional guarantees and proposed that section 116 should operate not only when the very purpose of a law was the restriction of religious freedom, but also in the case of laws that had this effect.[46]

The third constitutional rights provision, section 117, has been somewhat more successful. Its convoluted protection from discriminatory State legislative or executive action was interpreted very narrowly to offer a minimalist protection from discrimination in one State on the basis of residence in another State — until 1989.[47] In *Street v Queensland Bar Association*,[48] the High Court relied on section 117 to invalidate Rules of the Queensland Supreme Court that restricted the right to practice of barristers resident in other Australian States. Members of the Court adopted a broad construction of the section on the basis that it was designed to protect individual liberty. They were prepared to take into account the practical effects of a law. The tone of the judicial discussion in *Street* about this right was uncharacteristically robust and enthusiastic, perhaps because members of the Court could readily identify with the breach of the right at stake.

IMPLIED RIGHTS

In the 1990s, some members of the High Court expressed (albeit in a restrained way) frustration with the paucity of constitutional rights protections through the implication of rights in the constitutional text. For example, in 1992 the High Court acknowledged that the Constitution requires some degree of freedom of political communication.[49] An implied freedom was based on the system of representative government enshrined in the Constitution, and the fact that free political communication was essential to the government's proper functioning. In later cases, the implied right was used as a basis for a defence to defamation actions.[50] The scope of the right was limited in 1997 to communications relevant to the system of government directly established by the Constitution — in other words, federal and Territory government alone.[51]

Other High Court decisions have sketched a right to legal equality.[52] Chief Justice Gleeson has argued that a right to due process may be constructed from section 71 of the Constitution, which vests Commonwealth judicial power in the High Court and courts of federal jurisdiction, combined with the principles of separation of powers and independence of the judiciary.[53] The High Court has also occasionally recognised common law rights, such as the right to counsel.[54] But generally implied rights do not have a firm status in our constitutional fabric. The changing membership of the High Court makes them vulnerable to reinterpretation and indeed to evaporation. And there are controversial questions of legitimacy at stake. The Chief Justice of the High Court, Murray Gleeson, has cautioned against judicial adventurousness with implications from the constitutional text. In his 2000 Boyer Lectures, the Chief Justice said:

> Whatever room there may be for debate about the meaning of what the framers of the Constitution said, either expressly or by implication, and subject to the possibility of constitutional change, we are bound by their choice not to say certain things. We can interpret what they provided, and make implications from what they said where that is appropriate. But if they remained silent upon a matter, and legitimate techniques of interpretation cannot fill the gap they have left, then we are bound by their silence.[55]
>
> ...
>
> Silence, whether deliberate or not, binds us conclusively. Concern about how much importance attaches to what the founders meant to say may be trivial compared to the importance of the subjects that they left untouched.[56]

THE HINDMARSH ISLAND CASE

The inadequate protection of rights contained in Australia's Constitution and the wary approach of the High Court when human rights are at issue are well illustrated in the *Hindmarsh Island* case.[57] This case arose out of a controversy over the building of a bridge linking Hindmarsh Island in South Australia to the mainland. Some Aboriginal groups protested the bridge's construction on the basis that it breached laws protecting Aboriginal heritage. The Commonwealth government then enacted a special law, the Hindmarsh Island Bridge Act 1997, to override the heritage protection legislation, and construction of the bridge began. The constitutional basis for the Act was section 51 (xxvi) of the Constitution, which gives the Commonwealth the power to legislate with respect to 'the people of any race for whom it is deemed necessary to make special laws'. The main constitutional issue in the case was whether the power to make special laws on racial grounds included laws that treated one racial group *less* favourably than another. The Commonwealth government, supported by the governments of the Northern Territory, South Australia and Western Australia, argued that the Commonwealth could, if it chose, enact laws that singled out a particular racial group for adverse treatment. There is little doubt — when considering discussions from the constitutional conventions of the 1890s — that the constitutional drafters intended this to be the case. The plaintiffs contended that section 51 (xxvi) should be interpreted in the light of modern standards, which would require special laws based on race to be for the *benefit* of particular racial groups.

There was a startling exchange during the High Court proceedings that sums up the breadth of the Commonwealth's arguments. Justice Kirby asked the Commonwealth Solicitor-General:

> Can I just get this clear in my mind, is the Commonwealth's submission that it is entirely and exclusively for the Parliament to determine the matter upon which the special laws are deemed necessary ... or is there a point at which there is a justiciable question for the Court? I mean, it seems unthinkable that a law such as the Nazi race laws could be enacted under the race power and that this Court could do nothing about it.

The Solicitor-General responded:

> Your Honour, if there was a reason why the Court could do something about a Nazi law, it would, in our submission, be for a reason external to the races power. It would be for some wider, over-arching reason.[58]

The final outcome of the High Court's decision — that the Hindmarsh Island Bridge Act was within Commonwealth legislative power — left the question raised by Justice Kirby unresolved. The Court was effectively split on the issue. But the fact that the Commonwealth's argument could be seriously put and considered by the High Court, and the fact that it was supported by three members of the current High Court bench, illustrate the inadequate nature of our constitutional order with respect to the protection of rights. The text of the Constitution apparently reveals no 'overarching reason' to prevent a government from legislating to establish a system of racial discrimination, or indeed from systematically violating any human right.

LEGISLATIVE PROTECTION OF RIGHTS

If the Australian Constitution is silent about all but a handful of rights, what other forms of protection exist in the Australian legal system? In 1973 Senator Lionel Murphy, the Labor Attorney-General in the first Whitlam government, introduced a Human Rights Bill into the Australian Parliament as a precursor to constitutional change. The draft legislation was based on the UN International Covenant on Civil and Political Rights of 1966 (ICCPR) and sought to bind both federal and State governments. Within the Bill, federal laws inconsistent with the Human Rights Bill were deemed to be inoperative unless they expressly declared that they would operate in spite of the legislation. State laws inconsistent with the Human Rights Bill would be automatically invalid. The Bill drew storms of protest, most particularly based on the claim that it would diminish States' rights. Eventually the Bill was allowed to lapse.

In 1981 the Coalition Fraser government passed the Human Rights Commission Act, which provided administrative remedies for violations of some internationally-recognised rights by the Commonwealth government. The legislation created a Human Rights Commission and authorised it to examine federal laws for consistency with international human rights standards. The Commission could also receive complaints, but its ultimate sanction was to report the result of its investigations to the Commonwealth Parliament. The rationale for this modest protective system was that the most effective protection of human rights rested on drawing the legislature's attention to breaches.

A further legislative attempt to enact a bill of rights was made in 1983 by the Labor Attorney-General, Senator Gareth Evans. He proposed a much watered-down version of the Murphy Human Rights Bill, providing for judicial interpretation to favour constructions of laws that promoted human rights. The Attorney-General described the draft law as 'a shield not a sword' with respect to the protection of rights.[59] The legislation did not allow any direct challenge to laws by a person affected by them, although it was possible to seek a declaration that a particular law was inconsistent with the Bill of Rights. A strong attack was made on the proposals on the premise that the law would diminish State legislative power. The controversy meant that in the end the draft law was not introduced into Parliament.

In 1985 the Labor Attorney-General, Lionel Bowen, introduced yet another version of an Australian Bill of Rights into Parliament. The draft legislation was narrower still than the Evans Bill. The Bowen Bill applied only to federal laws and excluded all State laws from its scope. Despite its modest form, the Bill attracted such intense opposition from politicians from all political parties that it was allowed to lapse.

The following year, the Commonwealth Parliament enacted the Human Rights and Equal Opportunity Commission Act. This created a new institution, the Human Rights and Equal Opportunity Commission (HREOC), to replace the Human Rights Commission whose legislation automatically expired after five years. The ICCPR is appended to the legislation, but the rights it sets out (apart from those relating to race, sex and disability discrimination)[60] are implemented in a tenuous way. HREOC has jurisdiction only in relation to Commonwealth laws.[61] Its functions are to examine legislation for consistency with human rights standards and to report its findings to the Attorney-General.[62] HREOC may also attempt to conciliate human rights issues.[63] Its power, with leave of the court, to intervene in judicial proceedings where there is a human rights issue[64] has been used with some effect. However, in 1998 an attempt was made to curb the power to intervene by making HREOC subject to approval by the Commonwealth Attorney-General.[65] This draft legislation was ultimately withdrawn, but it emphasises the vulnerability of the statutory system to being whittled away by politicians.

The success of HREOC in bringing human rights issues into the public consciousness over the years has been due to the high calibre and fearlessness of its Presidents and Commissioners, rather than to the structure of, and mandate granted by, the legislation. More often than not, however, HREOC's recommendations to Parliament to remedy breaches of human rights have been ignored. The disdain and hostility with which HREOC's inquiry into the 'stolen generation' of Aboriginal children[66] was treated by the Commonwealth government illustrate the weakness of our current system in responding to major human rights issues.

Improving Australia's rather threadbare protection of human rights seems far from the political agenda. Two recent initiatives, however, suggest that the issue may be revived. In October 2000 the Australian Democrats released for comment an Australian Bill of Rights Bill. The draft law, based on the ICCPR, would apply to both State and Commonwealth governments. The Labor Shadow Attorney-General, Robert McClelland, has also signalled an interest in a statutory bill of rights, albeit one that would be applicable only to Commonwealth laws.[67]

There have been two unsuccessful attempts to amend the Constitution to insert rights guarantees. The first was in 1944 and related to post-war reconstruction. The amendments proposed by the Labor government of the time would only have operated for five years after the end of the war. A provision preventing State and federal governments from abridging freedom of speech was included in order to mollify those who feared that the Labor government might impose a socialist program. The amendments also extended the guarantee of religious tolerance in section 116 to the States.[68]

The second attempt was in 1988. In a hasty and politically clumsy bid to achieve constitutional change during the bicentenary of European settlement in Australia, the Labor government submitted four proposals to referendum, including some relating to rights drawn from the report of an expert Constitutional Commission.[69] The amendments relating to rights were very modest. Among other things, they would have extended to the States the right to trial by jury and to freedom of religion.[70] The proposals were defeated by a huge margin, with only 31 per cent of the electorate approving the rights provisions.

A CENTURY OF RELUCTANCE ABOUT RIGHTS

Since federation, Australian politicians have been very sceptical about the value of establishing guarantees of rights in the legal system. Two themes enliven this scepticism.

The first is the conflict between the protection of human rights and the preservation of States' rights. As we have seen, attempts to insert a modest catalogue of rights into the Australian Constitution foundered largely because of fears that guarantees of rights would limit the power of the States to restrict the privileges of non-Europeans. The spectre of States' rights was also an effective tactic against attempts in the 1970s and 1980s to introduce legislative catalogues of rights. The protection of States' rights remains a potent argument at the centenary of federation, with both major political parties apparently accepting that States and Territories should be free to enact legislation that breaches international human rights standards. The deployment of the rhetoric of States' rights in the debates over human rights in Australia has some resonance with the historiography of the American Civil War. Although contemporary documents indicate that both the North and the South regarded the institution of slavery as the cause of the war, Confederate politicians and some historians later denied that slavery was central to the conflict. They argued instead that the war was fought over the issue of States' rights to secede from the Union and the consent of the governed; in essence it was about the North's attack on the South's constitutional rights.[71] This 'Lost Cause' interpretation of the Civil War remains powerful today, allowing the South to view its defeat as a noble pursuit of liberty. The Australian invocation of the notion of States' rights as a counterpoint to human rights shares this revisionist quality.

This precedence accorded to States' rights over human rights has impoverished Australian social and political culture. The use of the word 'rights' in the slogan 'States' rights' obscures the reality that one major freedom sought by the Australian States over the last 100 years is that to deal unfettered with the human rights of its residents. In this sense, States' rights have often been pitted against the protection of human rights in Australia's history. A century after federation, such a notion of States' rights is inappropriate. We should carefully re-examine the way that we organise power in Australia and what the appropriate provinces for State power as opposed to national power are: we should be asking about the type of society we wish to live in and how we can best create this, rather than clinging to outmoded concepts of States' rights.

A second consistent basis for the Australian reluctance about rights has been the notion of parliamentary sovereignty inherited from the United Kingdom and the tradition of responsible government — the convention that the executive branch of government is kept in check by being answerable to the elected legislature — to protect individual rights. Sir Owen Dixon, perhaps the most influential Chief Justice of the Australian High Court, explained to a US audience in 1942 that a study of the US Constitution 'fired no [Australian constitutional drafter] with enthusiasm for the principle [of guarantees of rights]'. He went on:

> Why, asked the Australian democrats, should doubt be thrown on the wisdom and safety of entrusting to the chosen representatives of the people ... all legislative power, substantially without fetter or restriction?[72]

Sir Robert Menzies later offered another US audience a more detailed account of the protection of individual rights in the Australian political process:

> Should a Minister do something which is thought to violate fundamental human freedom he can be promptly brought to account in Parliament. If his Government supports him, the Government may be attacked, and, if necessary defeated. And if that ... leads to a new General Election, the people will express their judgment at the polling booths. In short, responsible government in a democracy is regarded by us as the ultimate guarantee of justice and individual rights.[73]

These sentiments are similar to those of many contemporary Australian politicians. Confidence in the parliamentary process to protect rights extends across the political spectrum. For example, in 2001 the NSW Labor Premier, Bob Carr, strongly attacked proposals for a bill of rights. He said:

> Parliaments are elected to make laws. In doing so, they make judgments about how the rights and interests of the public should be balanced. Views will differ in any given case about whether the judgment is correct. However, if the decision is unacceptable, the community can make its views known at regular elections. This is our political tradition. A bill of rights would pose a fundamental shift in that tradition, with the Parliament abdicating its important policy-making functions to the judiciary ... A bill of rights is an admission of the failure of parliaments, governments and the people to behave in a reasonable, responsible and respectful manner. I do not believe we have failed.[74]

So too, the Commonwealth Attorney-General, Daryl Williams, launched National Law Week in 2001 by criticising proponents of a bill of rights. He argued:

> We have a system of representative and responsible government, certain important constitutional guarantees, explicit protections in legislation including specialised human rights legislation, and protections in the common law. Our democratic institutions hold governments accountable. They limit potential abuses of power. They support a

democratic civil culture ... Parliaments make laws in this country. In doing so, they make decisions about how competing rights and freedoms, including those of the community at large, are to be balanced.[75]

This bipartisan faith in the convention of responsible government and the traditions of majoritarian parliamentary sovereignty to protect individual rights has not been justified in practice in Australia. Our legal history is littered with laws that discriminated against particular groups: the legal framework that allowed Aboriginal children to be taken from their families; the laws that made homosexuality a criminal offence; the laws that institutionalised discrimination against women; immigration laws that effectively restricted entry into Australia to particular races. Australian Parliaments today tolerate laws that allow mandatory sentencing of children, laws that treat 'boat people' who apply for refugee status more harshly than other refugee applicants, laws that sanction discrimination against women and laws that allow degrading treatment of prisoners. Political majorities and the majority of the community are unlikely to be concerned if the rights of an unpopular minority group are infringed. Indeed, the major political parties in Australia typically agree on the groups whose rights can be restricted: for example, prisoners and refugee applicants. Legislation restricting the rights of these groups usually has bipartisan support. The claim that 'robust parliamentary debate' operates to protect rights[76] has little empirical basis in Australian history. Indeed, recent research into the operation of the Commonwealth Parliament indicates the sharp diminution of the role of the legislature in all areas of policy development.[77] Political debate is strictly governed by party allegiance, and rare attempts by individual politicians to pursue human rights issues have almost always been muzzled.

The claim that Parliament is the proper protector of human rights reflects the power of the ideology of utilitarianism in Australian public life.[78] Utilitarianism views the aim of political society as the achievement of the greatest happiness of the greatest number: a utilitarian would thus be anxious to ensure that the majority's will, however expressed, prevailed at all times, and would design constitutional systems to achieve this. Utilitarian philosophers typically reject the idea of individuals as bearers of rights because this implies that individual or minority interests may on occasion take precedence over those of the majority.

Thus the philosopher Jeremy Bentham, the 'father' of utilitarianism, referred scathingly to the French Declaration on the Rights of Man of 1798 as 'bawling upon paper'. For him, the French National Assembly was an institution of the people, and it was therefore contradictory to assert that there was a need to place limits on its power. If the greatest happiness of the greatest number was the measure of right and wrong and the proper aim of a constitution, the determination of the majority contained in a legislative act must be conclusive. The idea of natural or inalienable rights was, Bentham wrote, 'rhetorical nonsense — nonsense upon stilts'. He went on: 'from imaginary laws, from the laws of nature ... come imaginary rights, a bastard brood of monsters, "gorgons and chimeras dire"'.[79]

Utilitarianism rests on a judgment about the aggregate interests of a community. It has no concern with identifying the interests of minority groups who may be worst off in society. For example, if we used average life expectancy of all Australians as the basis for public policy, we would miss the significantly lower rates of life expectancy of indigenous peoples and the differences in male and female rates. As Martha Nussbaum has pointed out:

> Average utility is an imprecise number, which does not tell us enough about different types of people and their relative social placement. This makes it an especially bad approach when we are selecting basic political principles with a commitment to treat each person as an end ... What is more, utilitarians typically aggregate not only across distinct lives but also across distinct elements of lives. Thus, within the total or average utility will lie information about liberty, about economic well-being, about health, about education. But these are all separate goods, which to some extent vary independently and ... we should not give up one of them simply to achieve an especially large amount of another.[80]

The utilitarian approach places the rights of vulnerable minority groups at the mercy of the will of the majority, as well as making particular rights subject to trading-off with others. A richer understanding of democracy involves acknowledging that there are some rights that are so basic to human dignity that they should be taken out of the political arena and given special protection. Laurence Tribe has argued that constitutional protection of rights allows the limitation of future freedom of action 'in order to reap the rewards of acting in ways that would elude [political majorities] under pressure of the moment'.[81]

IS CONSTITUTIONAL AMENDMENT THE ANSWER?

Given the inertia of the last century, or perhaps more accurately the hostility provoked by talk of rights protection in Australia, a suggestion of constitutional amendment to include guarantees of rights may appear both quixotic and naïve. It has been argued that, as the foundational document of our public life, the Constitution should only be rarely amended. Jeremy Webber, for example, urges the exercise of 'constitutional reticence' in matters of social values because they are likely to be very complex and because constitutionalising such issues excludes broad participation of citizens in the discussion.[82] Webber argues that a constitution should provide a *process* for discussion, rather than a catalogue of substantive values.

I share Jeremy Webber's concerns about forcing public conversations about fundamental values into exclusively legal or constitutional frameworks. At the same time, I see the Australian Constitution as actively *excluding* most discussion in the area of human rights. It leaves such debates exclusively in the political realm, which is in a sense the least hospitable of all to proposals for the restriction of governmental power. In other words, in Australia we need a new framework or process to allow us to debate such issues of fundamental value: this issue is discussed further in Chapter 3.

Apart from the philosophical objections to constitutional amendment in Australia, there is also the political reality that, in Geoffrey Sawer's striking words, Australia is, constitutionally speaking, the 'frozen continent'.[83] A referendum is most unlikely to succeed without bipartisan support.

Given this history, is a proposal for explicit rights protection in our Constitution worth pursuing? I will examine the elements of such a proposal in Chapter 3, but for now I want to suggest that, from a human rights perspective, the past 100 years of federation demonstrate that we need to be more active in thinking about the protection of rights in our legal and constitutional order. The Australian judiciary has neither the text nor the temperament to compensate for the constitutional silence about rights. In order to avoid the centenary celebrations being a grand exercise in self-congratulation, we need to be aware of the gaps in our human rights architecture, and work to repair them for the new century.

2

THE INTERNATIONAL HUMAN RIGHTS SYSTEM

I have argued that there is a great silence in the Australian constitutional tradition with respect to the protection of human rights and urged a rethinking of our complacency in this area. I have not yet, however, examined what the term 'human rights' means. I want to argue that the international system of human rights protection created over the last century offers a useful translation of human rights norms that could be adapted and incorporated into our constitutional fabric. I do not want to suggest that international human rights law is a perfect blueprint for Australia, but rather that it is a useful starting point for discussions of constitutional reform.

EXPLAINING HUMAN RIGHTS

There is a vast philosophical literature on this topic, but I do not have the space or capacity to survey it in full. I take the term 'human rights' to mean the conditions necessary for people to live lives of dignity and value. Johan Galtung has captured this idea in his description of human rights as a safety net, the 'rock bottom of human existence'.[1] In other words, human rights are what we want to remove from the agenda of short-term politics.[2] They create 'a protective sphere for vital interests, which people need to persuade them that they may accept vulnerability, run risks, undertake adventures in the world, and operate as citizens and as people'.[3] I follow Immanuel Kant in believing that the claim to observance of human rights stems from the inherent dignity of the human person.[4]

The legal philosopher Ronald Dworkin has used the metaphor of a card game to explain the legal power of human rights. Although Dworkin's views have been developed in the context of the US Constitution, they are relevant also to understanding claims to human rights more generally. For Dworkin, politics can be seen as a card game, which is run along majoritarian, and thus utilitarian, lines. The collective preferences of the community as a whole normally determine its course. Rights can be seen as trumps in this political card game. They attach to individuals when, says Dworkin:

> ... for some reason, a collective goal is not a sufficient justification for denying them what they wish, as individuals, to have or to do, or not a sufficient justification for imposing some loss or injury upon them.[5]

Dworkin argues that rights protection is dependent on one or both of two beliefs: a commitment to human dignity suggestive of the injustice of treating a person in a manner that does not recognise membership of the human community; and a belief in the value of the political equality of all citizens.[6] Dworkin is not concerned with whether we accept these beliefs as eternal truths or simply as utilitarian postulates. For him, it is crucial that we accord the preservation of an individual's dignity and equality a paramount value, and regard their violation as beyond the reach of ordinary utilitarian justification. On this view, short-term social cost cannot be a barrier to the guarantee of individual rights.

It is important to note that Dworkin does not regard particular individual rights as absolute, so they are trumps only in a limited sense. He argues that if the exercise of an individual right creates 'a clear and substantial risk' of 'great damage to the person or property of others', a right may be abridged if no alternative means exist to prevent the damage.[7] Central to Dworkin's argument is the contention that competition between rights can only take place between the rights of individuals. An individual right can never be weighed against the rights of the majority, because rights are based on the position of an individual within a society.

ORIGINS OF THE INTERNATIONAL HUMAN RIGHTS MOVEMENT

The development of an international system of human rights law dates from the end of the Second World War and the founding of the United Nations in 1945. The idea that individuals have some form of basic rights is, however, much older. Indeed, traces of rights talk can be found in ancient Greek and Roman philosophy. For example, when Sophocles' Antigone defied Creon's command not to bury her slain brother, she said: 'But all your strength is mere weakness against the immortal unrecorded laws of God'.[8] Invoking the higher laws of the gods that required her brother's burial, Antigone used a rights-based argument. In China, the government of the Chin dynasty, founded 2200 years ago, operated with a belief in the fair treatment of all, irrespective of caste.[9] The third century BC inscriptions of the Indian emperor, Ashoka, emphasised tolerance and liberty as central values of a good society.

The rhetoric of freedom is also present in the writings of the Buddha, who explained *nirvana* as freedom from the miseries of life, achieved by the extinction of the phenomenal self, which is the source of desire and craving.[10] Later, the tradition of natural law as developed in Europe by St Thomas Aquinas and others had human rights elements, particularly the idea that there was a higher law above that of governmental authority. And in the 17th and 18th centuries, the writings of Locke, Montesquieu and Rousseau, which were translated into action by the French and American revolutions, promoted the idea that humans were born with certain inalienable rights and that violation of these rights by government justified the overthrow of the government.

Although there were vigorous attacks on the notion that individuals had rights simply by virtue of being human (for example, recall Jeremy Bentham's dismissal of talk of rights as 'nonsense upon stilts'), social movements, such as the anti-slavery campaign and the women's suffrage movement, kept the idea of basic rights alive at an international level. In the 20th century, leaders of resistance movements, such as Mahatma Gandhi, also invoked notions of rights in their struggles.[11]

All this time, however, international law remained largely detached from concerns of individual or group rights. The province of international law was considered to be the relationships *between* countries, not the relationship between a country and its population. The atrocities of the Holocaust before and during the Second World War finally prompted the international community to formally acknowledge its concern with nation-states' treatment of all individuals within their jurisdictions.

The Charter of the United Nations contains the first explicit recognition in international law that an individual is entitled to the observance of fundamental rights and freedoms. Among the purposes of the United Nations set out in Article 1 of the Charter is that of co-operation 'in promoting respect for human rights and fundamental freedoms for all'. Article 55 commits the United Nations to promote 'universal respect for, and observance of, human rights and fundamental freedoms for all without distinction as to race, sex, language or religion', and Article 56 provides that all members 'pledge themselves to take joint and several action in cooperation with the Organization for the achievement of the purposes set forth in Article 55'. While the Charter's provisions are couched in general language, there is no doubt that they impose a legal duty on member states to observe human rights.[12]

The Universal Declaration of Human Rights, adopted unanimously by the General Assembly of the United Nations in 1948, gave content to the undefined notion of fundamental human rights in the Charter. Although the Universal Declaration was not originally intended to be a formally binding instrument, it has quickly developed the status of an authoritative interpretation of the Charter. Together with the International Covenant on Civil and Political Rights (ICCPR) and the International Covenant on Economic, Social and Cultural Rights (ICESCR) — both adopted by the United Nations in 1966 — the Universal Declaration forms the so-called 'International Bill of Rights'. Quite apart from the specific treaty obligations contained in the Covenants, observance of many of the principles set out in the Universal Declaration and the Covenants is now generally considered to be required by customary international law binding on all nations.[13]

While the Universal Declaration and the Covenants deal with human rights generally, a variety of other instruments dealing with specific areas of human rights have been adopted internationally. Some deal with particular rights (for example, the Genocide Convention of 1948, the Convention on the Elimination of All Forms of Racial Discrimination of 1965, and the Convention Against Torture and Other Cruel, Inhuman or Degrading Treatment or Punishment of 1984), and some deal with particular categories of rights holders (for example, the Standard Minimum Rules for the Treatment of Prisoners of 1957, the Convention on the Elimination of All

Forms of Discrimination Against Women of 1979, the Convention on the Rights of the Child of 1989, and the Convention on the Protection of the Rights of All Migrant Workers and Members of their Families of 1990). The International Labour Organization, the United Nations Economic, Social and Cultural Organisation (UNESCO), and other specialised agencies of the United Nations have drafted and now administer a wide range of human rights instruments. There are also a number of significant regional human rights treaties, such as the European Convention on Human Rights of 1950, the Inter-American Convention on Human Rights of 1969, the African Charter of Human and Peoples' Rights of 1982, and the Arab Charter on Human Rights of 1994.

The international law of human rights is, then, a comparatively sophisticated and well-developed system. International human rights standards offer an understanding of Johan Galtung's notion of the 'rock bottom of human existence'. They offer a considerable range of human rights guarantees, from civil and political rights; to economic, social and cultural rights; to collective, or group, rights such as the right to self-determination. The catalogue of international human rights is, however, imperfect in a number of ways. It reflects the era of its drafting and contains some gaps, for example, with respect to the rights of indigenous peoples and the rights of women. While international human rights standards are often couched in general language, it is clear that the assertion of rights is not unlimited. Thus article 29 of the Universal Declaration of Human Rights states that limitations on rights are permissible:

> ... for the purpose of securing due recognition and respect for the rights and freedoms of others and of meeting the just requirements of morality, public order and the general welfare of a democratic society.

Implementation of the major UN human rights treaties is monitored by a system of specialist committees, which are discussed further in Chapter 3. International judicial or quasi-judicial bodies of differing structures and jurisdictions supervise compliance with the regional treaties.

The international system of human rights protection may have a long history, but as we see all the time, concern with human rights remains very controversial internationally because it conflicts with traditional notions of state sovereignty that accord states great freedom in their domestic, or national, activities. Economic and political considerations often take precedence over human rights on the international agenda. The very basis of human rights law is politically contentious because it imposes restraints on governmental action in the name of individual or minority autonomy. Both authoritarian and democratically-elected governments are subject to the constraints of human rights law. In this sense, human rights law is essentially non-utilitarian or counter-majoritarian because it provides protection for individuals, groups and minorities so that in certain defined contexts their interests are not always sacrificed to those of the government or political majority of the day.

CHALLENGES TO THE INTERNATIONAL HUMAN RIGHTS MOVEMENT

The international human rights movement has attracted many critics. One source of criticism has come from countries that have been the focus of human rights attention. These countries typically insist that international scrutiny of human rights constitutes interference with national sovereignty. This argument is difficult to reconcile with the principles of international law that remove matters of human rights observance from the purely domestic sphere. There have also been significant challenges to the claims to universality of human rights standards.

CULTURAL BIAS OF HUMAN RIGHTS STANDARDS

One such challenge has come from the 'South', or the developing world. It has been argued that the international law of human rights is effectively a Western construct. The former is ostensibly universal, critics say, but in fact it reflects the values of Western liberal culture — individualism over communitarianism, political and civil rights over economic and social rights. This type of attack has been particularly pronounced in the Asia-Pacific region. For example, in 1997 the Malaysian Prime Minister, Dr Mahathir, suggested that the Universal Declaration of Human Rights should be redrafted to take 'Asian values' into account. He attacked 'individuals in some developed countries [who] consider it their right to tell us how to rule our country'. He suggested that these individuals 'latch on to various causes such as human rights and the environment in order to reimpose colonial rule on us'.[14]

The debate has sometimes been characterised as one between a 'universalist' philosophy that imposes unvarying human rights standards on all cultures and a 'cultural relativist' position that argues that human rights should be shaped by the particular historical context of each nation.

However, as the Hong Kong-based jurist Yash Ghai has pointed out, rejection of human rights principles often comes from governments seeking to justify repressive practices. Minorities and local non-government organisations, by contrast, typically see international human rights standards as extremely important and useful benchmarks to measure governmental action.[15] Indeed, Dr Mahathir's former deputy, Anwar Ibrahim, has said:

> If we in Asia wish to speak credibly of Asian values, we too must be prepared to champion those ideals which are universal and belong to humanity as a whole. It is altogether shameful, if ingenious, to cite Asian values as an excuse for autocratic practices and denial of basic rights and civil liberties ... It is true that Asians place greater emphasis on order and societal stability. But it is certainly wrong to regard society as a kind of false god upon whose altar the individual must constantly be sacrificed.[16]

From an international law perspective, it is also striking that, despite the strong attack on human rights law as a vehicle for Western ideology, all the member states of the United Nations have become a party to at least one international human rights treaty. For example, all Asian countries are parties to the Convention on the Rights of the Child.

A different type of attack on the cultural bias of international human rights standards points to the metaphors used in implementing these international human rights norms. For example, Makau Mutua describes the subtext of the human rights movement as 'an epochal contest pitting savages, on the one hand, against victims and saviors on the other'.[17] The United Nations, non-government organisations and Western governments all tend to assume that human rights are at greater risk in developing countries, and present the West as the aspirational model of human rights observance.

HIERARCHIES OF RIGHTS

A second, and related, debate about international human rights law concerns the status of economic, social and cultural rights — rights such as the right to health, to education, to housing. Are these types of rights qualitatively different to civil and political rights, such as the right to be free from torture or the right to vote in elections? Some philosophers have argued that these two types of rights are fundamentally distinct. Civil and political rights are presented as negative rights because they simply restrain government action, while economic and social rights are viewed as positive rights requiring action and expenditure. For example, Maurice Cranston has attacked the idea of economic and social rights as irresponsible and preposterous, suggesting they will also water down the significance of civil and political rights.[18] Economic and social rights have been regarded with considerable suspicion, indeed hostility, by some Western countries. Thus the United States has refused to participate in the ICESCR.

The Universal Declaration of Human Rights contained civil and political rights *and* social, economic and cultural rights in the one document. It was initially assumed that a single treaty translation of the Universal Declaration would be prepared and would mirror the rights the Declaration contained. By the time the drafting of the treaty started in earnest, however, the Cold War had begun. The tensions of the Cold War were manifested in the human rights area through an ideological divide between the West and the socialist bloc countries. The West generally championed the centrality of civil and political rights, while the socialist countries promoted the value of economic and social rights. The outcome of these debates was the drafting of two separate treaties — the ICCPR and the ICESCR.

The assumption that these two categories of rights are fundamentally distinct is evident in the language of the two Covenants, particularly in the provisions relating to the duties to implement the terms of the treaty. The ICCPR states that treaty parties must undertake to ensure that people whose rights and freedoms have been violated have an effective remedy.[19] The ICESCR language is comparatively much weaker: a party 'undertakes to take steps … to the maximum of its available resources, with a view to achieving progressively the full realisation of the rights recognised … by all appropriate means …'.[20]

Some scholars have attacked the claim that civil and political rights are of a different quality to economic and social rights. They have pointed out that if civil and political rights are taken seriously, they are much more than just a restraint on government. For example, proper implementation of rights to be free from torture or from discrimination (classic civil and political rights) requires positive action and expenditure, such as education, monitoring and so on.[21] The bifurcation of the idea of human rights is nevertheless still an article of faith for major international players such as the United States, which has been unable to accept the ICESCR and argues consistently at international meetings that economic rights have no international status. On the other hand, at the Vienna World Conference on Human Rights in 1993 there was a consensus that the correct approach was to regard all categories of rights as inter-dependent and indivisible. Australia officially supports this approach at the international level, although it is reluctant to accord group or collective rights the same status as other human rights. For example, the Australian government's official *Human Rights Manual* gives less prominence to group rights than other forms of rights.[22]

The legacy of the bifurcation of categories of rights in the international system has created a gap in the monitoring of human rights. Most of the major international governmental and non-governmental institutions interested in human rights focus on civil and political rights, such as illegal detention and torture. Deaths by malnutrition or disease and lives spent in poverty are equally human rights concerns, but are rarely analysed in these terms. The structural adjustment programs imposed on debtor countries by the international monetary institutions have impinged on rights to health, education and housing; structural adjustment typically requires reduction of spending in the public sector and privatisation of many social services. The activities of the World Trade Organisation (WTO) have also affected economic, social and cultural rights. The WTO's focus on abstract economic markets has allowed it to ignore the implications of its decisions for human rights, such as the right to health care.[23]

CRITIQUE OF RIGHTS DISCOURSE

A third type of challenge to the language of human rights has come from post-modern critics, building on earlier Marxist critiques of rights. It has been argued, for example, that while recourse to the language of rights may add a rhetorical flourish to a claim, this provides only an ephemeral polemic advantage. Rights talk can thus mask the need for political and social change. The Brazilian jurist Roberto Unger has contended that invocation of rights may give a false appearance of the necessity and the unchangeability of the social order. An invocation of rights obscures the political and controversial nature of all of our decisions about social life and gives an appearance of progress where none has been made.[24]

Observers of the international human rights system offer a variation of this critique. For example, Costas Douzinas presents a damning portrait of the actors in the human rights movement — 'triumphalist column writers, bored diplomats and rich international lawyers ... whose experience of human rights violations is confined to being served a bad bottle of wine'.[25] He argues that the language of human rights has lost its revolutionary edge and has become co-opted into supporting the state.

Over the past decade a lively feminist critique of human rights has developed. Many different perspectives contribute to this critique. One regular theme suggests that the international human rights standards developed in the last century tend to respond to rights violations typically sustained by men.[26] Issues such as violence against women, which are at epidemic levels all around the world, have not been traditionally regarded as breaches of human rights because they do not fit neatly into the paradigm of international human rights.

Indigenous peoples have also criticised the absence of attention to their situation in the human rights canon. The provisions in the International Bill of Rights are not designed to acknowledge the particular claims and disadvantages of minority indigenous groups. For example, international human rights law offers little protection to people whose primary allegiance is to their land. The continuing difficulties surrounding the drafting of a Declaration on the Rights of Indigenous Peoples illustrate the limited horizons of the official human rights system.

While these criticisms contain much force, the imaginative, transcendent power of human rights claims must be balanced against them. Human rights are a framework for debate over basic values and conceptions of a good society. Rights discourse offers a recognised vocabulary to frame political and social wrongs. Martha Minow has identified problems in denying rights discourse to marginalised groups: 'I worry about criticising rights and legal language just when they have become available to people who had previously lacked access to them. I worry about those who have, telling those who do not, "you do not need it, you should not want it"'.[27] Rights talk can often seem naïve and unpragmatic and is capable of intense manipulation: however, its power relies on a basic commitment to justice and rightness.[28]

RELIGIOUS PERSPECTIVES ON HUMAN RIGHTS

Yet another form of challenge to the international human rights movement has come from religious traditions. While ideas about human rights may have once been connected with religions, the international law of human rights has been largely detached from religious world views. Indeed, the *travaux préparatoires* of the Universal Declaration of Human Rights reveal that there was a proposal by Brazil and the Netherlands to include a reference to a deity in the preamble and article 1, to the effect that 'human beings are created in the image of God ... [and] are endowed by nature with reason and conscience'. This proposal was rejected because of objections that this would offend those nations without a natural law tradition and also non-believers.[29]

Human rights law does not ignore religion as an aspect of peoples' lives. It recognises a right to freedom of religion, and discrimination on the basis of religion is prohibited by international law.[30] In 1981, after 20 years of debate, the UN General Assembly adopted a Declaration on the Elimination of All Forms of Intolerance and of Discrimination based on Religion or Belief, and this may one day form the basis of a treaty on religious intolerance. The UN Commission on Human Rights has also appointed a Special Rapporteur on Religious Intolerance.

The engagement of human rights law and religion has been by and large at a procedural level, concerned with freedom of religion as an aspect of freedom of speech and thought. Even this limited engagement has been controversial, because some religious traditions cannot accept the idea of freedom to choose a religion. Indeed, Saudi Arabia abstained from the vote adopting the Universal Declaration on Human Rights precisely because the Declaration endorsed freedom of religion and belief.[31] In any event, human rights law has resisted explicitly endorsing the substance of any particular religious tradition.

If human rights law has not engaged explicitly with religious traditions, what have religious traditions made of human rights? In one sense, human rights and religion are intimately, if ambivalently, related, in that religions provide a transcendent perspective by revealing a dimension of human life over and above the social and political order. Religions set a limit to the power of the collectivity and the state, since in a religious context the state cannot profess to be the unitary source of all authority. The tensions between religion and the state run, for example, through European history. There are the debates between Socrates and the Athenian state, between the Church and temporal rulers about the things that are Caesar's and the things that are not Caesar's in the Middle Ages, and about the role of individual conscience in radical Protestantism in the 16th and 17th centuries.

From this perspective, one might think that religious traditions would be the natural champions of human rights. But none of the great religions of the Book — Christianity, Islam and Judaism — have endorsed human rights ideas unequivocally. Their texts speak of obligations and duties rather than rights and their histories contain many examples of their discrimination, intolerance and oppression — crusades, jihads, inquisitions and ostracisms of many sorts.[32] For example, the Roman Catholic Church did not condemn slavery until the late 19th century and it took almost 2000 years to acknowledge at the Second Vatican Council that there was a right to freedom of religious belief and practice.[33] Straight after the Second World War, Christian and Jewish groups actively participated in the development of international human rights norms, but at the institutional level this interest seemed to wane over time.[34]

The most problematic and controversial issue in the engagement of religion and the international human rights movement has been the issue of women's rights. A basic principle of human rights law, recognised in all general human rights treaties, is the norm of non-discrimination on the basis of sex. However, all the major religious traditions discriminate against women in various ways: for example, women are typically precluded from becoming priests, rabbis, mullahs or bishops. This discrimination against women is usually explained by religious tradition. Thus the Catholic Church relies on the fact that Jesus did not include women among the twelve Apostles to justify the exclusion of women from the priesthood.

Some religious scholars have argued that discrimination against women is not actually required by religious texts and scriptures, but this research has had little impact on religious practices. Generally, and very successfully, religious traditions have attempted to quarantine their traditions from human rights law, particularly in the area of women's rights.

A good example of this is the reservations made by Islamic states to the Convention on the Elimination of All Forms of Discrimination against Women. Typical of these reservations is that of Egypt. With respect to article 16 of the Women's Convention, which requires that states observe equality between men and women in all matters concerning marriage and family relations, Egypt's reservation states that this matter must be subject to Islamic *Shari'a* law, the body of scriptural interpretation of the *Qur'an*. Israel, India and the United Kingdom have also entered reservations to the Convention in order to protect the laws of religious communities generally from the scope of the treaty.

The claim by religious traditions that the right to practice religion should be given priority over other human rights is also evident in local contexts. For example, in Australia many religious institutions lobbied successfully to gain exemption from the State and federal laws prohibiting sex discrimination. Thus the Commonwealth Sex Discrimination Act 1984 specifically excludes from its provisions sex discrimination in the ordination or appointment of priests and ministers or members of a religious order[35] and 'any … act or practice established for religious purposes, where the act or practice conforms to the doctrines, tenets or beliefs of that religion or is necessary to avoid injury to the religious susceptibilities of followers of that religion'.[36] In 2000 Australian church groups reacted strongly to HREOC guidelines designed to prevent religious discrimination by church groups administering a government employment service. The churches persuaded the Commonwealth government that the guidelines breached the right to religious freedom. They argued that their right to practise a religion should be given priority over individual rights to employment and equal treatment.[37]

Is the idea of human rights incompatible with religious belief? Should one set of commitments trump the other? As a beginning point there needs to be much closer dialogue between the two. How could religious traditions respond to the international human rights system? One method is the development of a 'human rights hermeneutic'.[38] Thus in the context of Islam, the Sudanese jurist Abdullahi An-Na'im has described a process of reinterpretation of the sources of Islamic tradition in a way that both preserves legitimacy and is consistent with human rights norms. He has argued that we need to understand that religious traditions reflect a historically-conditioned interpretation of scripture, influenced by social, economic and political circumstances.[39]

For example, An-Na'im says, with respect to the strictures on the role of women in the *Shari'a*, we need to note that equality between women and men at the time of the development of the *Shari'a* in the Middle East would have been inconceivable. By analysing the *Shari'a* principle of *qawama* — the guardianship and authority of men over women — it can be seen to be based on assumptions that have little relevance today: that men are stronger than women and that men financially support women. The principle, An-Na'im has suggested, should not therefore retain its legitimacy. A similar analysis could apply to the scriptures of Christianity that are used to justify the exclusion of women from the priesthood or higher church offices.[40]

We also need to be alert to the political uses of claims of religious culture. We need to ask whose culture is being invoked, what the status of the interpreter is, in whose name the argument is advanced and who the primary beneficiaries are.[41] In other words, whose interests are served by arguments based on religion and what hierarchy is created? At the international level, religious traditions are used in a complex way to preserve the power of elite groups of men. The appeal to the sanctity of religion is considerably reduced if it is being used to bolster the existing distribution of power and privilege.

THE VALUE OF INTERNATIONAL HUMAN RIGHTS STANDARDS

I have sketched some of the challenges made to international human rights standards from a range of perspectives. These indicate some of the baggage carried by the concept of human rights. Another critical weakness is that the international human rights system relies almost completely on national implementation for its effectiveness, as the international implementation procedures are weak and cumbersome. Countries that are willing to subscribe to international treaties nevertheless tend to regard international scrutiny of their human rights practices as a violation of their sovereignty, as we see regularly in Australia. Moreover, human rights standards are couched in broad and general language and do not provide many easy solutions to controversial issues.

For all these limitations, however, I want to suggest that the international law of human rights is a valuable source of norms to import into Australia's constitutional fabric. Respect for human rights is based on a belief in human dignity and the international standards are a useful, if flawed, translation of the conditions for human dignity. In many areas, international law reflects an international consensus about the elements of Galtung's 'rock bottom of human existence' and can provide a set of principles that enable people to live lives of full human value and worth. Of course, mere statements of rights will not deliver progressive social change and are not a ready panacea for oppression and domination. But the international language of rights nevertheless contains transformative potential. Human rights law offers a vocabulary and structure in which claims by marginalised groups can be formulated; it also allows dialogue on difficult issues of human existence. Peter Van Ness has said that human rights law allows 'continually changing, negotiated understandings of that which it is most essential to protect in order to defend and to enhance our common humanity ... [T]he standards are not perfect: they are simply the best that have been identified and agreed upon thus far. Nothing more'.[42]

3

PROTECTING HUMAN RIGHTS IN AUSTRALIA

In the last chapter, I argued that the international system offers a valuable, if imperfect, catalogue of human rights that can guide us in the attempt to design changes to Australia's constitutional architecture. In this chapter, I will ask what effect the international law of human rights has had thus far on Australian legal culture. I will also explore the models for change offered by Canada, South Africa and the United Kingdom.

INTERNATIONAL HUMAN RIGHTS LAW AS PART OF AUSTRALIAN LAW

A traditional principle in our legal system holds that domestic law is not impacted by international law unless it is specifically incorporated through legislation or judicial pronouncement. As we have seen, Australia is a party to all the major UN human rights treaties; but this has not had much direct impact on Australian law. Indeed, Australia appears to be Janus-faced with respect to human rights treaties. The internationally-oriented face basks in the international status it receives from being a party to the treaties, while the nationally-turned face is more diffident, reluctant to acknowledge the domestic implications of its international obligations. Australia has thus managed to remain relatively aloof from the scope of international human rights law.

LEGISLATION

In Chapter 1, I sketched the various failed attempts to incorporate the provisions of the International Covenant on Civil and Political Rights (ICCPR) by legislation into Australian law. The major international human rights standards that have been formally translated into Australian law are those relating to some forms of discrimination. Successive Australian governments have argued that other international human rights principles are protected adequately under existing State and federal laws. It is important to note that the constitutionality of the federal anti-discrimination legislation depends largely on the Commonwealth's power to legislate with respect to 'external affairs'.[1] In this sense, the Australian protection of human rights is critically dependent on the international legal system.

In 1975 the Commonwealth government enacted the Race Discrimination Act, which implemented — at least in the federal sphere — many of the provisions of the Convention on the Elimination of All Forms of Racial Discrimination. The legislation is administered through the Human Rights and Equal Opportunity Commission. A critical weakness of the Act is its vulnerability to amendment in light of changing government policies. For example, the Commonwealth Native Title Act 1993 was amended in 1998 to create 'legal certainty' for governments and non-indigenous title-holders to land. Among other things, the amendments allowed validation of the extinguishment of native title but not of other forms of land title. The overall effect was to discriminate against indigenous title-holders in favour of non-indigenous land-owners, a discrimination in clear breach of the Convention. The UN Committee on the Elimination of Racial Discrimination found the Native Title Amendment Act 1998 was incompatible with Australia's treaty obligations,[2] but this conclusion was rejected by the Australian government.

The Commonwealth Sex Discrimination Act 1984 was designed to implement Australia's obligations under the Convention on the Elimination of All Forms of Discrimination Against Women 1979. The translation of the treaty into Australian law is, however, incomplete. The Sex Discrimination Act, for example, contains significant exemptions that preclude the principle of non-discrimination on the basis of sex applying in all contexts. These exemptions include various acts performed under statutory authority;[3] the work of charities, religious, voluntary and sporting bodies;[4] orders of industrial tribunals;[5] and combat duties in the defence forces.[6] The legislation is also at the mercy of government policies. For example, in 2000 the Howard government introduced legislation to amend the Sex Discrimination Act to allow discrimination between women in the context of using assisted reproductive technologies.[7] The proposed amendments would allow the States to prevent single women and women in homosexual relationships from having access to these technologies.

The third form of discrimination prohibited by Commonwealth law is that based on a mental or physical disability. The Disability Discrimination Act 1993 offers limited protection to people with a disability in certain contexts. Other forms of discrimination, such as discrimination on the basis of religion, political belief, or sexuality, are not prohibited under federal law, although State and Territory laws offer a varying range of protections for them.

Overall, Australian legislation with respect to human rights is limited and patchy. In the process of regular periodic reporting by Australia on its implementation of its international obligations, the UN human rights treaty-monitoring bodies have identified many gaps and inadequacies in our legal framework.[8] Some of these are referred to below.

JUDICIAL ATTITUDES TO HUMAN RIGHTS LAW

Australian courts have shown sporadic interest in international human rights law. For example, members of the High Court in *Mabo v Queensland (no 2)* emphasised the significance of international law in the development of the common law. Justice Brennan described the relationship in this way:

> The common law does not necessarily conform with international law, but international law is a legitimate and important influence on the development of the common law, especially when international law declares the existence of universal human rights.[9]

Justice Brennan argued that if a common law doctrine was based on an outdated notion of international law (such as the Australian land tenure system built on the international legal principle of *terra nullius*), the common law could lose its legitimacy. For this reason, the High Court developed a new notion of native title that recognised indigenous property rights in land.

In 1995 the High Court identified a significant role for human rights treaties in administrative law in *Minister for Immigration and Ethnic Affairs v Teoh*.[10] At issue in this case was the status of the UN Convention on the Rights of the Child, a treaty ratified by Australia but not specifically incorporated into Australian law. A majority of the Court held that entry into a treaty by Australia creates a legitimate expectation that the government will act in accordance with the treaty provisions whether or not the treaty has been implemented in Australian law. In other words, administrative decision-makers should consider all relevant treaties to which Australia is a party in reaching their decisions and if decision-makers propose to make a decision inconsistent with a treaty obligation, they should allow persons affected by the decision to make submissions on this point. For this reason, the Court decided that the decision to deport Mr Teoh, a convicted drug trafficker with a number of dependent children resident in Australia, should have considered Australia's obligation to give weight to the best interests of children under the Convention on the Rights of the Child. Chief Justice Mason and Justice Deane stated that the influence of international legal principles on the common law would depend on factors such as the nature and purpose of the international legal norm, its degree of international acceptance and its relationship with existing principles of domestic law. Although the Court emphasised the need for a cautious approach to the use of international treaties in developing the common law, the *Teoh* decision to require the decision-maker to turn her mind to the Convention obligations (but not necessarily to give them precedence) caused an uproar. Politicians condemned it as an inappropriate judicial excursion into the political realm. The Minister for Foreign Affairs, Gareth Evans, and the Attorney-General, Michael Lavarch, immediately sought to override the impact of the decision in an unprecedented formal statement. They asserted that Australia's ratification of a treaty could not give rise to a legitimate expectation that administrative decision-makers would take the treaty obligations into account.[11] This position was repeated and strengthened in 1997 by the Howard government. A joint statement by the Attorney-General, Daryl Williams, and the Minister for Foreign Affairs, Alexander Downer, stated:

> The Government is of the view that [the Teoh principle that entry into a treaty created a legitimate expectation that the treaty obligations would be followed] is not consistent with the proper role of Parliament in implementing treaties in Australian law.[12]

Both the Keating and Howard governments have (as yet) unsuccessfully attempted to legislate to overcome the effect of the decision.[13]

Justice Michael Kirby has been a consistent exponent of the significance of international human rights law in the Australian legal system. His judgments as President of the NSW Court of Appeal indicate a keenness to consider international standards in the interpretation of Australian law.[14] While it is an accepted principle of statutory interpretation that legislation should be interpreted as far as possible in conformity with international law in the case of ambiguity, unambiguous language is usually assumed to override international law.

Since his appointment to the High Court, Justice Kirby has sought to broaden the influence of international law, particularly in the area of constitutional interpretation. In *Newcrest Mining* in 1997, Justice Kirby said: 'To the full extent that its text permits, Australia's Constitution, as the fundamental law of government in this country, accommodates itself to international law, including insofar as that law expresses basic rights'. He also introduced the idea that the Constitution spoke not just to the people of Australia but also to the international community.

Justice Kirby's dissent in the *Hindmarsh Island* case, discussed in Chapter 1, accepted the plaintiff's argument that the Commonwealth's power to legislate with respect to race should be read in light of international standards of non-discrimination. Justice Kirby spoke of an interpretative principle to the effect that, where the Constitution is ambiguous, the High Court 'should adopt the meaning which conforms to the principle of universal and fundamental rights rather than an interpretation which would involve a departure from such rights'.[15] Indeed, he referred to a 'strong presumption' that the Constitution is not intended to violate fundamental human rights and human dignity, implying that the Constitution should be interpreted in light of international law regardless of whether or not an ambiguity could be identified.

Justice Kirby's approach to international human rights law is, however, considered controversial,[16] and is not generally shared by the Australian judiciary. Judicial interpretation is, therefore, no compensation for the Australian legal system's silences about human rights. The Federal Court's decision in *Nulyarimma v Thompson* in 1999[17] highlights the limits of Australian law in this respect. An Aboriginal plaintiff argued that government policy and legislation on native title contained in the 1998 'Ten Point Plan' and the Native Title Amendment Act 1998 constituted acts of genocide. The central issue in this case was whether a prohibition on genocide was part of Australian law. Although Australia ratified the Convention on Genocide in 1949, no legislation has since been enacted to give the international legal standard domestic force. The plaintiff in *Nulyarimma* argued that the prohibition of genocide was a norm of customary international law and, as such, should be considered a principle of Australian law. This argument has a strong jurisprudential basis,[18] but it was rejected by a majority of the Federal Court bench, who regarded the principles of customary international law as outside Australian law. In dissent, Justice Merkel found that a prohibition on genocide was part of the common law, but he did not find it applicable to the native title policy or laws.

DIRECT RECOURSE TO THE INTERNATIONAL HUMAN RIGHTS SYSTEM

The international system offers various mechanisms for monitoring implementation of human rights standards. In 1991 and 1993 Australia accepted the right for individuals in Australia to complain directly to three of the UN treaty-monitoring bodies (the Human Rights Committee under the ICCPR,[19] the Committee on the Elimination of Racial Discrimination under the Convention on the Elimination of all Forms of Racial Discrimination,[20] and the Committee against Torture under the Convention Against Torture)[21] about violations of treaty obligations.[22] The right to make an individual communication or complaint at the international level can only be exercised when all domestic legal avenues for redress have been exhausted. This requirement ensures that the international system cannot be used in a frivolous way: it can only be invoked where Australian law offers no adequate remedy for a violation of an internationally recognised right.

By May 2001, 57 complaints against Australia had been lodged with the UN treaty-monitoring bodies under the three treaties. Eight complaints had gone through all the procedural steps and had been determined on their merits. In three cases, the treaty bodies had found violations of international obligations. The first of these cases, filed in 1992, was that of Nicholas Toonen, a Tasmanian gay activist who complained that the Tasmanian Criminal Code's criminalisation of male homosexual acts violated his right to privacy under article 17 of the ICCPR and his right to non-discrimination under article 26.[23] The Human Rights Committee considered his arguments and those of the Australian and Tasmanian governments and concluded that there was a breach of article 17. The Committee recommended to the Australian government that the Tasmanian law be repealed. The outcome of the Human Rights

Committee's recommendation was that the Commonwealth government enacted the Human Rights (Sexual Conduct) Act of 1994 to effectively overturn the Tasmanian law. In the end, the Tasmanian Parliament repealed the relevant provisions of the Criminal Code.

A second successful communication against Australia was made by a Cambodian 'boat person' held at Port Hedland Detention Centre.[24] The complainant, known as A, argued that the length and conditions of his detention violated his rights under articles 9 and 14 of the ICCPR. The Human Rights Committee found that there had been breaches of article 9 relating to the right not to be arbitrarily detained and the right to test the legality of detention in judicial proceedings. The response to the views of the UN Committee was dismissive: the Australian government simply stated that it did not accept the Committee's interpretation of article 9.

In 1998 a Somali national, Mr Elmi, invoked Australia's obligations under the Convention against Torture to argue to the Committee against Torture that he should not be deported to Somalia because he was likely to be tortured upon return.[25] The Committee upheld his complaint and the Australian government refrained from the deportation.

Does Australia's experience with direct access to the UN human rights treaty-monitoring bodies suggest that the international arena is an adequate safety net for human rights breaches in Australia? Can we thereby avoid the rocky road of constitutional change to incorporate protection of human rights into Australian law?

Direct recourse to the international human rights system is limited in a number of ways. First, the UN complaint system is very slow and cumbersome. The human rights committees all operate on a part-time basis and are over-worked and under-resourced. It can take up to four years for the merits of a complaint to be addressed. Moreover, the communications are dealt with on the basis of written arguments from the complainant and the country concerned and the committees never have the opportunity to hear from the parties or their advocates in person. Furthermore, the outcome of the UN committee system's consideration of a complaint is the adoption of 'views' on whether or not an internationally-recognised right has been breached. While the views of the committees constitute an authoritative interpretation of the treaties, there is little formal pressure on governments to accept interpretations adverse to their perceived interests.

A second problem with reliance on the international system of human rights alone is that it will always be vulnerable to the claim that international standards are somehow foreign and thus lack legitimacy in regulating action in Australia. These claims of foreignness and illegitimacy are often quite unfairly (indeed shamelessly) manipulated by the media and by politicians. After all, if Australia actually becomes a party to a treaty and thus voluntarily accepts the treaty obligations, why should we not expect the government to fulfil the treaty provisions? Even if these claims — based on the idea that using international human rights standards to measure the legality of governmental action in Australia somehow impinges on our national sovereignty — do not hold up logically, they remain politically powerful and persuasive. For example, in 2000 the Prime Minister, Mr Howard, reacted angrily to suggestions that the UN Secretary-General might criticise the Northern Territory's mandatory sentencing laws as inconsistent with Australia's human rights obligations. Mr Howard was reported as saying that 'Australia would make its own moral judgments and would not be told what to do by outsiders'. He continued: 'I'm not going to cop this country's name being tarnished in the context of a domestic political argument'.[26] Mr Howard's reaction was echoed by some State and Territory Labor politicians.

The rise of the One Nation political party in the late 1990s has exacerbated suspicion of international human rights standards. One Nation has used the United Nations as a stalking horse, portraying it as responsible for many of the evils of globalisation and the evisceration of Australian sovereignty. Pauline Hanson, for example, has attacked the work of the United Nations in the area of indigenous rights as well as the anti-tariff policies of the World Trade Organisation. The One Nation attack has perhaps pressured many Australian politicians to demonstrate their patriotism by criticising the United Nations, particularly in the area of human rights. The power of the anti-international human rights rhetoric is evident in a joint press statement of August 2000 by the Minister for Foreign Affairs, Alexander Downer, the Minister for Immigration, Philip Ruddock, and the Attorney-General, Daryl Williams, reporting on the results of a closed review of Australia's interaction with the UN human rights treaty system.[27] The review was prompted by criticism of Australia's periodic reports by the human rights treaty-monitoring bodies. The Ministers announced a policy of distancing Australia from the UN system, due to these bodies' alleged propensity to criticise democratically-elected governments. At the same time, the Ministers announced an intention to work at the international level to improve the effectiveness of the treaty bodies. The press statement referred to the need for a 'complete overhaul' of the treaty-monitoring bodies 'to ensure adequate recognition of the primary role of democratically-elected governments and the subordinate role of non government organisations; [and] to ensure that committees and individual members work within their mandates'. It stated that the government would 'adopt a more robust and strategic approach to Australia's interaction with the treaty committee system both to maximise positive outcomes for Australia and enhance the effectiveness of the system in general'. The rather truculent tone of the statement was reinforced by references to a future 'economical and selective approach' in Australia's reporting to and representation at UN human rights forums, and a decision that Australia would not sign or ratify a new avenue for individual communications, the Optional Protocol to the Convention on the Elimination of Discrimination against Women.

It seems, then, that recourse to international human rights standards somehow triggers a deeply isolationist streak in the Australian psyche. I do not want to suggest that Australia is especially recalcitrant or alone in this: we see the same tendency in many powerful global players. For example, China's 1991 White Paper on human rights firmly rejected the notion that its protection of human rights could be properly subject to international scrutiny.[28] Similarly, the United States has remained quite aloof from the international human rights treaty system. It took the United States almost 40 years to agree to become a party to the Genocide Convention. When it finally ratified the ICCPR, it did so with a list of reservations almost as long as the treaty itself; for example, asserting the right to execute minors convicted of serious crimes.[29] The United States is not a party to the ICESCR, the Women's Convention or the Children's Convention.

Paradoxically, politicians and commentators who tap into the Australian vein of isolationism with respect to international human rights systems and standards also generally resist the creation of a home-grown system of rights protection. For example, Mr Howard has insisted that the common law is capable of responding to any issue of human rights. He firmly rebuffed a proposal by former Prime Minister Malcolm Fraser for an Australian Bill of Rights on the grounds that it would prompt unnecessary litigation.[30] As we have seen, however, Australian law offers very haphazard protection of human rights and it is precisely this quality that has led to international scrutiny. One way to reduce international criticism of our human rights record would be to create a truly Australian system of human rights protection. This would mean that human rights issues would be debated and decided in Australia with a fuller appreciation of our historical and cultural context.

MODELS FOR CONSTITUTIONAL CHANGE

I have argued that the Australian legal system does not offer an adequate system for the protection of human rights and that the 'safety net' offered by the processes of the international legal system has many weaknesses. What are the alternatives? I want to consider models offered in three other countries whose legal systems are not too dissimilar to our own to see what we lessons we can draw from them.

CANADA

The Canadian constitutional system has many affinities with the Australian system. We are both collections of former British colonies that decided to federate but retain a direct imperial connection. Our judicial traditions are similar. For almost 100 years the Canadian Constitution — the British North America Act of 1867 — contained no system of human rights protection. As in Australia, a system of judicial review of the constitutionality of legislation operated haphazardly to provide some protection to individual rights. In 1960 Prime Minister Diefenbaker introduced legislation to create a statutory bill of rights, the Canadian Bill of Rights. The legislation was largely a result of concern about the expansion of executive power and the influence of the international human rights movement.

The Bill of Rights set out a catalogue of civil and political rights, including rights to due process of law, equality before the law and equal protection, and freedom of speech and religion. The rights were to be used in the interpretation of federal legislation but not the legislation of the Canadian Provinces. The Bill of Rights also authorised the Minister for Justice to examine all proposed legislation for consistency with the rights set out and to report any inconsistency to the Canadian House of Commons. In the 22 years of the Bill's life such a report was made only once. The Bill of Rights allowed two major exemptions to its terms: a federal statute could expressly declare that it was to operate notwithstanding the Bill of Rights and the Canadian War Measures Act was exempted from the scope of the Bill of Rights.

The Canadian Bill of Rights had little practical force: a total of 30 cases involving the legislation came before the Canadian Supreme Court in 22 years. Only once was a federal statute declared inoperative under the terms of the Bill of Rights.[31] The Canadian courts seemed to be uncomfortable and at sea with the Bill of Rights and they developed a raft of doctrines to limit its scope and to give primacy to the notion of parliamentary sovereignty. For example, the Supreme Court adopted what became known as the 'frozen concepts' principle — in other words, the Bill of Rights was taken to deal only with rights that were recognised at the time of its enactment.[32] In other instances, the Supreme Court argued that the Bill of Rights was only relevant in cases of ambiguous legislation: if the legislation in question clearly and expressly violated human rights, the Bill of Rights could not be invoked, as the assumption must be made that it was Parliament's will to breach human rights.[33]

In 1982 the Canadian Constitution was patriated through the UK Parliament's adoption of the Canada Act. At the same time, due to the great commitment and energy of the Prime Minister, Pierre Trudeau, a Charter of Rights and Freedoms was inserted into the Constitution. The Charter set out various categories of rights drawn from national and international sources: fundamental freedoms including conscience and religion, thought, expression and association; democratic rights (the right to vote, the maximum duration of legislatures and their minimum annual meeting times); mobility rights; legal rights (procedural rights in criminal matters and the right to an interpreter in all proceedings); official language rights and the educational rights of minority language groups. The Charter also affirmed existing aboriginal and treaty rights of the Indian, Inuit and Métis populations. The Charter rights were made enforceable by the courts, which can grant remedies for infringement of rights as they consider appropriate and just. Because of the Charter's constitutional status, any law inconsistent with the Charter has no force or effect.

The Canadian Charter has two particular provisions that limit its scope. The rights and freedoms it contains are subject 'to such reasonable limits prescribed by law as can be demonstrably justified in a free and democratic society'.[34] The second, inserted at the last minute as the price of the Provinces' agreement to the Charter, allows any Canadian legislature to exclude legislation from most of the Charter's operation by express declaration for (renewable) five-year periods.[35] This 'notwithstanding' clause has been rarely invoked by the Provinces and never by the federal government.

The Charter has changed the character of Canadian constitutional law. It has brought a raft of major social and political issues before the Canadian Supreme Court. For example, the right to equality in section 15 of the

Charter has been broadly interpreted as a substantive right and not just a right to equal treatment: it prevents discrimination against groups subject to stereotyping, historical disadvantage and social prejudice.[36] Not surprisingly, the Supreme Court's decisions have regularly provoked great controversy. The criticism has come from all sides. Some argue that the Court is now overtly political; some criticise the Court for its failure to advance real social justice in Canada; some attack the very design of the Charter, which they assert does not touch the real causes of social injustice. Thus Joel Bakan points out that a right to freedom of association cannot protect workers from unemployment and the increasing mobility of capital, the real threats to rights to organise, bargain collectively and strike.[37] Also, various groups and corporations have been able to use the Charter to avoid legislative restrictions designed to prevent them from harming and exploiting others. Corporations have piggybacked on the notion of individual rights. For example, in the *Big M* case a corporation charged with breaching a statute prohibiting large businesses from opening on a Sunday successfully argued that the law violated the freedom of religion of individuals who belonged to religions that observed the Sabbath on days other than Sunday.[38] Prohibitions on anti-Semitic hate speech have been held to violate the right to freedom of expression.[39]

The Canadian example reminds us that a set of constitutionally entrenched rights cannot by itself deliver social justice. It can be one tool among many social, economic and political influences contributing to social justice. It is a mechanism to promote a multi-layered discussion and dialogue between the institutions of government and the people on the basic conditions of a good life.

SOUTH AFRICA

The South African Constitution of 1996, which replaced an interim Constitution that came into force in 1994, is a second recent model for a national system of rights protection. The Constitution was drafted over two years by the newly elected multi-racial Parliament and involved extensive public consultation. Like the interim model, the 1996 Constitution included a Bill of Rights; the provisions of this Bill may only be restricted (as in the Canadian Charter) by limitations that are reasonable and justifiable in an open and democratic society based on human dignity, equality and freedom.[40] The South African Bill of Rights applies to all law and to all the organs of state and directly in private relations.[41]

The South African Bill of Rights is striking among the three models I am describing for its broad coverage of rights. It includes the standard civil and political rights as well as economic and social rights such as access to housing, health care, food, water and security. It also includes rights such as that to a healthy environment and also various forms of property rights, including the right to compensation if property is expropriated.

There have been some major human rights decisions under the South African Bill of Rights. One has required that immigration law treat same-sex partners of permanent South African residents in the same way as heterosexual spouses.[42] Another case, *Makwanyane*, decided under the interim Constitution, declared the death penalty unconstitutional because it violated human dignity, the right to life, the right not to be punished cruelly and inhumanely and the right to equal protection of the law.[43]

Of particular interest have been decisions of the South African Constitutional Court interpreting constitutional economic and social rights. The first, *Soobramoney*, involved the denial of ongoing dialysis treatment to a man suffering renal failure on the basis that there were not enough resources to give such treatment to all patients and that treatment should be reserved for patients who were able to have a kidney transplant.[44] The Court held that the right of access to health care was subject to the availability of resources. It did not see itself as appropriately second-guessing decisions made about the availability of dialysis by the hospital based on its allocated budget.

Grootboom, decided in October 2000, suggests quite a different approach to economic and social rights. A group of 500 children and 400 adults who were squatting on land in the Western Cape brought a case under the Constitution challenging their eviction. They argued that the South African government was required to provide them with adequate basic shelter or housing under the Bill of Rights. The South African Constitutional Court unanimously decided that the Bill of Rights required the state to devise and implement a program to realise progressively the right of access to reasonable housing.[45] Given the crisis situation with so many people living in intolerable conditions, the Court held that the programs in place were clearly inadequate. The Court looked to the parallel provisions in the ICESCR and to international jurisprudence on the right to housing. It decided that there was no doubt that economic, social and cultural rights were justiciable and that the government was required to act to fulfil them. The Court ordered the government to devise and implement a program within available resources to realise progressively the right of access to adequate housing.

UNITED KINGDOM

The third model for rights protection I want to consider is that of Australia's constitutional parent, the United Kingdom. The Human Rights Act 1998 is also the most recent model, having come into operation on 3 October 2000.[46] Until that time the most useful legal mechanism for the protection of human rights in the United Kingdom was the capacity of individuals to bring cases before the European Court of Human Rights under the European Convention on Human Rights of 1950 (ECHR). By the end of the 1990s, the United Kingdom had been found in breach of the Convention in over 50 cases.

The Human Rights Act gives the ECHR considerable legal status, although it does not directly incorporate the ECHR into British law. The Act employs a range of mechanisms to import the international standards into national law. First, the Act requires that all primary legislation (statutes) and subordinate legislation (regulations made under statutes) are, if possible, to be read and given effect to in a way that is compatible with the ECHR.[47] The interpretation of the ECHR by the European Commission and Court of Human Rights in Strasbourg must be taken into account by UK courts.[48] Second, courts simply cannot apply incompatible subordinate legislation. If it is impossible to interpret primary legislation compatibly with the ECHR, courts may make a 'declaration of incompatibility'.[49] Third, all public authorities (including courts and tribunals) must, if possible, act in a way that is compatible with the ECHR.[50] Public authorities are defined to include 'any person certain of whose functions are functions of a public nature'.[51]

The Human Rights Act has been termed 'the most significant formal redistribution of political power in the United Kingdom since 1688'.[52] However, the Human Rights Act is carefully designed to avoid encroaching directly on the traditional principle of parliamentary sovereignty. Parliament itself is not bound to act compatibly with the ECHR. The judiciary cannot declare primary legislation incompatible with international human rights standards to be invalid. The idea is that a formal declaration of incompatibility will place pressure on Parliament to amend the legislation.[53] It has been said that this mechanism establishes a dialogue between the judiciary, Parliament and the executive about the scope and nature of human rights and that the tripartite structure creates a space for the public also to participate in the debate about rights.[54]

There are already signs that the Human Rights Act is altering British legal culture. For example, a Scots court decision found that temporary sheriffs did not constitute 'independent and impartial tribunals' as required by the ECHR[55] because of their limited security of tenure.[56] The first Declaration of Incompatibility of legislation was made in March 2001. The English High Court held that provisions of the Mental Health Act 1983 were incompatible with the ECHR[57] because they required detained patients to prove that they were not mentally ill before a tribunal could order their release.[58] This reversal of the onus of proof breached the right to liberty and security of a person. Other decisions have concerned the operation of the criminal law. The distribution of a manual for public servants about the impact of the Human Rights Act on their work indicates the significant changes necessary to administrative operations.[59]

LESSONS FOR AUSTRALIA

What lessons for Australia can we draw from the three models I have just described? To address this question, I will focus on three issues: procedure for reform, the institutional shape for rights protection and the nature of rights to be protected.

PROCEDURE FOR REFORM

The three models I have set out suggest a variety of procedures to introduce rights into the Australian Constitution. At one end of the spectrum is the South African model: the adoption of a totally new constitution after massive political upheaval and extensive community consultation. Canada is an example of the two-stage procedure: first a statutory bill of rights and then, after a period of adjustment, the introduction of constitutional guarantees. The third case study, the United Kingdom's Human Rights Act, gives new local force to an existing international human rights treaty system.

The dramatic South African constitutional changes were of course prompted by massive political changes, the move from the era of apartheid and minority white government to majority black rule. It is difficult to imagine a parallel set of circumstances in Australia and I think we are unlikely to have the chance to begin all over again. We must work with what we have.

The British example suggests another type of approach: tying domestic rights protection to an existing international one. Australia is not a party to the European Convention on Human Rights, so the appropriate parallel procedure may be to legislate to require Australian courts to take into account the standards and the jurisprudence of the UN human rights system. This may not be as useful as the European system has been in the United Kingdom. The UN scheme does not operate as a proper judicial system. Its human rights committees are part-time institutions, without the resources or mandate to produce considered legal opinions on the basis of full argument about all the issues by the parties to a dispute. Nevertheless, a legislative requirement that Australian courts take the international treaty standards into account would be an advance on the present situation.

The most appropriate model for Australia may well be a version of the Canadian two-stage procedure: a statutory scheme of rights protection followed by constitutional entrenchment. This approach was recommended by the Australian Law Reform Commission in its report on Equality before the Law in 1994.[60] However, as the Canadian experience indicates, a statutory Bill of Rights may be no real guide at all as to how a constitutional system of rights protection will work. For 22 years, the Canadian Bill of Rights was effectively useless in protecting rights. Perhaps the way ahead is for Australia to begin with a statutory bill of rights, capable of relatively easy amendment, but to have a clear timetable for consideration of constitutional reform.

INSTITUTIONAL ARCHITECTURE

What is the best institutional architecture or design for human rights protection? The three models I have sketched all rely on an independent judiciary to interpret rights, although the British legislation carefully assigns the final word on rights to Parliament and the Canadian Charter contemplates legislative override of its provisions. All these jurisdictions also have systems for parliamentary scrutiny of draft legislation to ensure its consistency with human rights standards. It is often argued in Australia that the interpretation of a bill of rights is an inappropriate task to assign to an unelected body of judges; that it is not only anti-democratic because there is no accountability, but that making decisions on great moral, social or economic issues is often beyond the expertise of judges with their narrow legal training and backgrounds and should be left to legislators. This argument has been put forcefully by Frank Brennan.[61] From his observation of the US Supreme Court deciding cases on the US Bill of Rights, Frank

Brennan argues against constitutional entrenchment of a broad set of rights. He views Parliament as the proper institution to oversee the protection of rights and proposes a Senate Committee for Rights and Freedoms to scrutinise draft legislation in light of a Charter of Espoused Rights and Freedoms.

We should not assume, however, that Parliaments perfectly reflect the views of the majority. Electoral processes do not always result in governments who represent majority views on every issue. For example, on the very issue of protection of rights, an Australian National University survey found 72 per cent of citizens to be in favour of some form of bill of rights, with 54 per cent believing that rights were not well protected in Australia; 79 per cent of politicians, however, considered rights to be properly protected. Fifty-nine per cent of citizens regarded the courts as the appropriate final arbiter on questions of rights, while only 23 per cent of legislators agreed.[62] Even if politicians accurately mirrored majority views, this does not make them natural protectors of individual rights. Politicians may be accountable in one, short-term, sense to their electorate at each election, but with respect to issues of human rights their accountability is in reality rather weak. Politicians have little interest in making decisions that may upset the majority by protecting possibly unpopular minority group rights. In this sense, political majorities can often tacitly connive in the oppression of minority groups.

A critique of judicial scrutiny of human rights from a different direction argues that judges are too closely involved in the political process to be capable of effective protection of minorities. Mark Tushnet, for example, challenges the popular image of the US Supreme Court as a champion of the oppressed. He has pointed out that, in the US context, judicial and legislative attitudes to major social issues do not greatly differ.[63] Tushnet also contends that the quality of political decisions on particular issues is likely to be superior to that of judicial decisions. This is because decisions made by a legislature tend to be concrete rather than abstract, susceptible to negotiation and compromise rather than cast in absolute terms.[64]

Tushnet's study of US constitutional politics may offer some response to those who regard judicial monitoring of human rights as anti-democratic. The Australian system for judicial appointments is, however, not so overtly political as that of the United States, and Australian judges may not so closely track political trends. In any event, as I have argued, protection of human rights cannot be justified by a utilitarian approach, that is, as a task that will promote the greatest happiness of the greatest number. We have to take a much longer-term view of what makes a good and just society, including protecting the rights of minorities. The Australian judiciary is at least immune to the pressures of courting immediate popularity, a useful quality in the area of human rights. While I share the concern about the narrow perspective of the legal profession when it comes to social and moral questions, at the end of the day I nevertheless think that protection of rights is best overseen by a relatively independent judiciary, supported by a demanding system of parliamentary scrutiny of draft legislation and the possibility (discussed below) of legislative override of judicial decisions. The judiciary is a very conservative force, however, and its members tend to be drawn from social elites: white, private-school-educated men. Giving the judiciary a role in rights protection would make issues of a broader-based judicial selection critical. It would also mean that people like me who teach law students should ensure that we educate our future judges so that they are better equipped to deal with issues of human rights.

In any event, the current Australian constitutional system already accords considerable power to judges to review and invalidate legislation. The Commonwealth Parliament has always been constrained in its legislative powers by the terms of the Constitution and the power of interpreting the constitutional language is assigned to the High Court. While our judiciary usually presents the task of judicial review as an intrinsically legal, as distinct from a political, undertaking, the distinction between law and politics is inevitably deeply blurred in such cases. No clear line exists between legal and political decision-making, and the politics of judicial choice between rival interpretations of words cannot be eradicated. If our constitutional system has survived this significant power of judicial review for the last century, it is not obvious why broadening the grounds on which the power can be exercised would automatically undermine Australian democracy. The role of the judiciary would be to hold the government to its obligation to respect human rights, not to draw up detailed policy.

A striking feature of both the Canadian and British models is that they leave some scope for the legislature to enact laws that are contrary to human rights standards. In the Canadian case, this requires explicit acknowledgment that the legislation should operate 'notwithstanding' the Charter of Rights and Freedoms. This technique may be a useful one in an Australian context: it would preserve the ultimate power of Parliament to decide the nature of our laws, but provide considerable moral pressure on the legislature to act consistently with human rights standards.[65] The possibility for legislative override of judicial decisions also responds to concerns about the relative skills of the legislature and judiciary in balancing conflicting rights in concrete cases. A Canadian jurist has described the effect of the Charter as avoiding a 'contest of political and judicial wills' and encouraging 'an on going multi-layered constitutional conversation with Parliament and between Parliament and courts on the scope and meaning of fundamental human rights and the importance and justification of legislative objectives when these conflict with rights'.[66]

DEFINITIONS OF PROTECTED RIGHTS

The final issue on which our three models can shed some light is the type of rights that should be covered in an Australian catalogue of rights. The British model is a straightforward domestic translation of international standards. It is confined to a set of civil and political rights. The Canadian and South African models are a mix of some rights drawn from the UN human rights treaties and some rights that respond to the particular national context: the Canadian Charter's special attention to language rights, for example, reflects Canada's significant francophone population; the South African Constitution's references to people dispossessed of their land during the apartheid era respond to a major local issue.

In the Australian case, it may be least controversial to rely on already accepted international statements of rights such as set out in the ICCPR and the ICESCR, which have an established international jurisprudence to aid interpretation. On the other hand, our particular national context may require some more tailored rights — such as specific indigenous rights — that are largely ignored in the international instruments. Also, we may query the value of all the international catalogue of rights, whose formulations reflect the time of their drafting in the 1950s and 1960s. One way may be to use the international standards for the first phase of statutory rights protection and then to move to adjust them to become a truly Australian set of rights at the moment of constitutional amendment.

All the Australian models of bills of rights so far produced have focused on civil and political rights alone. For example, George Williams has suggested that the first step would be to protect 'a few core rights', such as the right to vote, the right to freedom of expression and the right to be free from discrimination on the basis of race or disability.[67] I support a broader

Australian bill of rights that would also encompass economic, social and cultural rights. The distinction between the two categories of rights is in many ways a contingent and artificial one. If human rights are concerned with the conditions of a worthwhile human life, rights to health, to housing and to education are as integral to human dignity as the right to vote.

An objection often made to economic and social rights in national legal systems is that these rights are not justiciable in the same way as civil and political rights and would require courts to become embroiled in political and economic issues. Indeed, the inclusion of economic and social rights in the 1996 South African Constitution was challenged as a violation of the framework principles set out in the 1994 interim Constitution, on the grounds that these rights were not 'universally accepted fundamental rights' and that they would require the judiciary to decide on budgetary matters, thus breaching the principle of separation of legislative, executive and judicial powers.[68] The South African Constitutional Court rejected this challenge. It did not regard the task of protecting civil and political rights as qualitatively different to that of economic and social rights. The Court noted that the proper observance of the former category of rights may have similar budgetary implications to protection of the latter. It said that '[a]t the very minimum, socio-economic rights can be negatively protected from improper invasion'.

A related and important issue is whether non-governmental actors should be bound by rights guarantees. At the very least, private entities carrying out public functions, such as privately-run prisons, should be bound to protect rights, as under the United Kingdom's Human Rights Act. There appears to be no reason in principle, however, why all private persons and entities should not be required to act consistently with human rights standards.

Australian politicians have begun to counter discussion about rights with the language of responsibilities or duties. Indeed, the government is currently proposing to rename HREOC as the Human Rights and Responsibilities Commission. A notion of responsibility to promote human rights is, of course, an integral aspect of the international system.[70] The assumption behind the recent Australian discussion, however, appears to be different. It seems to be that claims of rights are frivolous or reckless if they are not seen as implying a responsibility to act in particular ways. There is an element of a bargain here: you may have the right to education but you must contribute towards the cost; you may have the right to apply for refugee status but you must join the proper queue for applications. While there may be political mileage in this approach and while it may be appropriate in some policy contexts, it is quite distinct from the understanding of human rights for which I have argued.[71] Human rights are the product of the notion of human dignity. Claims to human rights will always need to be balanced against those of other individuals or groups or those of the community generally and as a result may be limited in an appropriate way. But human rights do not need to be earned by good behaviour or performance of duties.

THE WAY AHEAD

I have argued that the centenary of federation is an appropriate time to contemplate constitutional change and renewal and also that the most urgent task is to devise an Australian system to protect human rights. We are now the only common law country in the world without such a system. This fact is not itself an argument for change, but the reality that the protection of rights is so low on the Australian political agenda indicates how far we still have to go. It seems ironic that Australia still clings to a 19th century British faith that Parliament is a natural and perfect protector of human rights when Britain itself has discarded this conviction.

It is easy to become overwhelmed and daunted by working for such a cultural and legal change. It will take time and energy and persistence and it may be only a later generation who see this come to fruition. I do not think we can sit back and wait for politicians to take the initiative. Indeed, in one sense, politicians are the very group that has least interest in restricting the power of Australian Parliaments. A public forum, such as that of the Constitutional Convention on the republic in 1998, is one place to begin the discussion.

In his poem, 'Everything Changes', Bertolt Brecht captures well the tenacity of tradition, the tantalising possibility of change and the optimism and energy required to achieve it:

Everything changes. You can make
A fresh start with your final breath.
But what has happened has happened. And the water
You once poured into the wine cannot be
Drained off again.

What has happened has happened. The water
You once poured into the wine cannot be
Drained off again, but
Everything changes. You can make
A fresh start with your final breath.[72]

APPENDIX A

THE AUSTRALIAN CONSTITUTION 1901
(EXTRACTS)

RIGHTS ALLOWANCES

80. The trial on indictment of any offence against any law of the Commonwealth shall be by jury, and every such trial shall be held in the State where the offence was committed, and if the offence was not committed within any State the trial shall be held at such place or places as the Parliament prescribes.

116. The Commonwealth shall not make any law for establishing any religion, or for imposing any religious observance, or for prohibiting the free exercise of any religion, and no religious test shall be required as a qualification for any office or public trust under the Commonwealth.

117. A subject of the Queen, resident in any State, shall not be subject in any other State to any disability or discrimination which would not be equally applicable to him if he were a subject of the Queen resident in such other State.

SOURCE The Australian Constitution
http://www.aph.gov.au/senate/general/constitution/

APPENDIX B

CANADIAN CHARTER OF RIGHTS AND FREEDOMS 1982

GUARANTEE OF RIGHTS AND FREEDOMS

1. The *Canadian Charter of Rights and Freedoms* guarantees the rights and freedoms set out in it subject only to such reasonable limits prescribed by law as can be demonstrably justified in a free and democratic society.

FUNDAMENTAL FREEDOMS

2. Everyone has the following fundamental freedoms:
   (a) freedom of conscience and religion;
   (b) freedom of thought, belief, opinion and expression, including freedom of the press and other media of communication;
   (c) freedom of peaceful assembly; and
   (d) freedom of association.

DEMOCRATIC RIGHTS

3. Every citizen of Canada has the right to vote in an election of members of the House of Commons or of a legislative assembly and to be qualified for membership therein.

4. (1) No House of Commons and no legislative assembly shall continue for longer than five years from the date fixed for the return of the writs of a general election of its members.

   (2) In time of real or apprehended war, invasion or insurrection, a House of Commons may be continued by Parliament and a legislative assembly may be continued by the legislature beyond five years if such continuation is not opposed by

the votes of more than one-third of the members of the House of Commons or the legislative assembly, as the case may be.

5. There shall be a sitting of Parliament and of each legislature at least once every twelve months.

MOBILITY RIGHTS

6. (1) Every citizen of Canada has the right to enter, remain in and leave Canada.

(2) Every citizen of Canada and every person who has the status of a permanent resident of Canada has the right
(a) to move to and take up residence in any province; and
(b) to pursue the gaining of a livelihood in any province.

(3) The rights specified in subsection (2) are subject to
(a) any laws or practices of general application in force in a province other than those that discriminate among persons primarily on the basis of province of present or previous residence; and
(b) any laws providing for reasonable residency requirements as a qualification for the receipt of publicly provided social services.

(4) Subsections (2) and (3) do not preclude any law, program or activity that has as its object the amelioration in a province of conditions of individuals in that province who are socially or economically disadvantaged if the rate of employment in that province is below the rate of employment in Canada.

LEGAL RIGHTS

7. Everyone has the right to life, liberty and security of the person and the right not to be deprived thereof except in accordance with the principles of fundamental justice.

8. Everyone has the right to be secure against unreasonable search or seizure.

9. Everyone has the right not to be arbitrarily detained or imprisoned.

10. Everyone has the right on arrest or detention
(a) to be informed promptly of the reasons therefor;
(b) to retain and instruct counsel without delay and to be informed of that right; and
(c) to have the validity of the detention determined by way of habeas corpus and to be released if the detention is not lawful.

11. Any person charged with an offence has the right
(a) to be informed without unreasonable delay of the specific offence;
(b) to be tried within a reasonable time;
(c) not to be compelled to be a witness in proceedings against that person in respect of the offence;
(d) to be presumed innocent until proven guilty according to law in a fair and public hearing by an independent and impartial tribunal;
(e) not to be denied reasonable bail without just cause;
(f) except in the case of an offence under military law tried before a military tribunal, to the benefit of trial by jury where the maximum punishment for the offence is imprisonment for five years or a more severe punishment;
(g) not to be found guilty on account of any act or omission unless, at the time of the act or omission, it constituted an offence under Canadian or international law or was criminal according to the general principles of law recognized by the community of nations;

(h) if finally acquitted of the offence, not to be tried for it again and, if finally found guilty and punished for the offence, not to be tried or punished for it again; and

(i) if found guilty of the offence and if the punishment for the offence has been varied between the time of commission and the time of sentencing, to the benefit of the lesser punishment.

12. Everyone has the right not to be subjected to any cruel and unusual treatment or punishment.

13. A witness who testifies in any proceedings has the right not to have any incriminating evidence so given used to incriminate that witness in any other proceedings, except in a prosecution for perjury or for the giving of contradictory evidence.

14. A party or witness in any proceedings who does not understand or speak the language in which the proceedings are conducted or who is deaf has the right to the assistance of an interpreter.

EQUALITY RIGHTS

15. (1) Every individual is equal before and under the law and has the right to the equal protection and equal benefit of the law without discrimination and, in particular, without discrimination based on race, national or ethnic origin, colour, religion, sex, age or mental or physical disability.

(2) Subsection (1) does not preclude any law, program or activity that has as its object the amelioration of conditions of disadvantaged individuals or groups including those that are disadvantaged because of race, national or ethnic origin, colour, religion, sex, age or mental or physical disability.

OFFICIAL LANGUAGES OF CANADA

16. (1) English and French are the official languages of Canada and have equality of status and equal rights and privileges as to their use in all institutions of the Parliament and government of Canada.

(2) English and French are the official languages of New Brunswick and have equality of status and equal rights and privileges as to their use in all institutions of the legislature and government of New Brunswick.

(3) Nothing in this Charter limits the authority of Parliament or a legislature to advance the equality of status or use of English and French.

17. (1) Everyone has the right to use English or French in any debates and other proceedings of Parliament.

(2) Everyone has the right to use English or French in any debates and other proceedings of the legislature of New Brunswick.

19. (1) Either English or French may be used by any person in, or in any pleading in or process issuing from, any court established by Parliament.

(2) Either English or French may be used by any person in, or in any pleading in or process issuing from, any court of New Brunswick.

20. (1) Any member of the public in Canada has the right to communicate with, and to receive available services from, any head or central office of an institution of the Parliament or government of Canada in English or French, and has the same right with respect to any other office of any such institution where

(a) there is a significant demand for communications with and services from that office in such language; or

(b) due to the nature of the office, it is reasonable that communications with and services from that office be available in both English and French.

(2)   Any member of the public in New Brunswick has the right to communicate with, and to receive available services from, any office of an institution of the legislature or government of New Brunswick in English or French.

21. Nothing in sections 16 to 20 abrogates or derogates from any right, privilege or obligation with respect to the English and French languages, or either of them, that exists or is continued by virtue of any other provision of the Constitution of Canada.

22. Nothing in sections 16 to 20 abrogates or derogates from any legal or customary right or privilege acquired or enjoyed either before or after the coming into force of this Charter with respect to any language that is not English or French.

MINORITY LANGUAGE EDUCATIONAL RIGHTS

23. (1) Citizens of Canada

(a) whose first language learned and still understood is that of the English or French linguistic minority population of the province in which they reside, or

(b) who have received their primary school instruction in Canada in English or French and reside in a province where the language in which they received that instruction is the language of the English or French linguistic minority population of the province,

have the right to have their children receive primary and secondary school instruction in that language in that province.

(2)   Citizens of Canada of whom any child has received or is receiving primary or secondary school instruction in English or French in Canada, have the right to have all their children receive primary and secondary school instruction in the same language.

(3)   The right of citizens of Canada under subsections (1) and (2) to have their children receive primary and secondary school instruction in the language of the English or French linguistic minority population of a province

(a) applies wherever in the province the number of children of citizens who have such a right is sufficient to warrant the provision to them out of public funds of minority language instruction; and

(b) includes, where the number of those children so warrants, the right to have them receive that instruction in minority language educational facilities provided out of public funds.

ENFORCEMENT

24. (1)   Anyone whose rights or freedoms, as guaranteed by this Charter, have been infringed or denied may apply to a court of competent jurisdiction to obtain such remedy as the court considers appropriate and just in the circumstances.

(2)   Where, in proceedings under subsection (1), a court concludes that evidence was obtained in a manner that infringed or denied any rights or freedoms guaranteed by this Charter, the evidence shall be excluded if it is established that, having regard to all the circumstances, the admission of it in the proceedings would bring the administration of justice into disrepute.

GENERAL

25. The guarantee in this Charter of certain rights and freedoms shall not be construed so as to abrogate or derogate from any aboriginal, treaty or other rights or freedoms that pertain to the aboriginal peoples of Canada including
    (a) any rights or freedoms that have been recognized by the Royal Proclamation of October 7, 1763; and
    (b) any rights or freedoms that now exist by way of land claims agreements or may be so acquired.
26. The guarantee in this Charter of certain rights and freedoms shall not be construed as denying the existence of any other rights or freedoms that exist in Canada.
27. This Charter shall be interpreted in a manner consistent with the preservation and enhancement of the multicultural heritage of Canadians.
28. Notwithstanding anything in this Charter, the rights and freedoms referred to in it are guaranteed equally to male and female persons.
29. Nothing in this Charter abrogates or derogates from any rights or privileges guaranteed by or under the Constitution of Canada in respect of denominational, separate or dissentient schools.
30. A reference in this Charter to a Province or to the legislative assembly or legislature of a province shall be deemed to include a reference to the Yukon Territory and the Northwest Territories, or to the appropriate legislative authority thereof, as the case may be.
31. Nothing in this Charter extends the legislative powers of any body or authority.

APPLICATION OF CHARTER

32. (1) This Charter applies
    (a) to the Parliament and government of Canada in respect of all matters within the authority of Parliament including all matters relating to the Yukon Territory and Northwest Territories; and
    (b) to the legislature and government of each province in respect of all matters within the authority of the legislature of each province.
    (2) Notwithstanding subsection (1), section 15 shall not have effect until three years after this section comes into force.
33. (1) Parliament or the legislature of a province may expressly declare in an Act of Parliament or of the legislature, as the case may be, that the Act or a provision thereof shall operate notwithstanding a provision included in section 2 or sections 7 to 15 of this Charter.
    (2) An Act or a provision of an Act in respect of which a declaration made under this section is in effect shall have such operation as it would have but for the provision of this Charter referred to in the declaration.
    (3) A declaration made under subsection (1) shall cease to have effect five years after it comes into force or on such earlier date as may be specified in the declaration.
    (4) Parliament or the legislature of a province may re-enact a declaration made under subsection (1).
    (5) Subsection (3) applies in respect of a re-enactment made under subsection (4).

SOURCE Canadian Charter of Rights and Freedoms 1982
http://laws.justice.gc.ca/en/charter/

APPENDIX C

SOUTH AFRICAN CONSTITUTION 1996

BILL OF RIGHTS

7. 1) This Bill of Rights is a cornerstone of democracy in South Africa. It enshrines the rights of all people in our country and affirms the democratic values of human dignity, equality and freedom.

(2) The state must respect, protect, promote and fulfil the rights in the Bill of Rights.

(3) The rights in the Bill of Rights are subject to the limitations contained or referred to in section 36, or elsewhere in the Bill.

APPLICATION

8. (1) The Bill of Rights applies to all law, and binds the legislature, the executive, the judiciary and all organs of state.

(2) A provision of the Bill of Rights binds a natural or a juristic person if, and to the extent that, it is applicable, taking into account the nature of the right and the nature of any duty imposed by the right.

(3) When applying a provision of the Bill of Rights to a natural or juristic person in terms of subsection (2), a court —

(a) in order to give effect to a right in the Bill, must apply, or if necessary develop, the common law to the extent that legislation does not give effect to that right; and

(b) may develop rules of the common law to limit the right, provided that the limitation is in accordance with section 36(1).

(4) A juristic person is entitled to the rights in the Bill of Rights to the extent required by the nature of the rights and the nature of that juristic person.

EQUALITY

9. (1) Everyone is equal before the law and has the right to equal protection and benefit of the law.

(2) Equality includes the full and equal enjoyment of all rights and freedoms. To promote the achievement of equality, legislative and other measures designed to protect or advance persons, or categories of persons, disadvantaged by unfair discrimination may be taken.

(3) The state may not unfairly discriminate directly or indirectly against anyone on one or more grounds, including race, gender, sex, pregnancy, marital status, ethnic or social origin, colour, sexual orientation, age, disability, religion, conscience, belief, culture, language and birth.

(4) No person may unfairly discriminate directly or indirectly against anyone on one or more grounds in terms of subsection (3). National legislation must be enacted to prevent or prohibit unfair discrimination.

(5) Discrimination on one or more of the grounds listed in subsection (3) is unfair unless it is established that the discrimination is fair.

HUMAN DIGNITY

10. Everyone has inherent dignity and the right to have their dignity respected and protected.

LIFE

11. Everyone has the right to life.

FREEDOM AND SECURITY OF THE PERSON

12. (1) Everyone has the right to freedom and security of the person, which includes the right —

(a) not to be deprived of freedom arbitrarily or without just cause;

(b) not to be detained without trial;

(c) to be free from all forms of violence from either public or private sources;

(d) not to be tortured in any way; and

(e) not to be treated or punished in a cruel, inhuman or degrading way.

(2) Everyone has the right to bodily and psychological integrity, which includes the right —

(a) to make decisions concerning reproduction;

(b) to security in and control over their body; and

(c) not to be subjected to medical or scientific experiments without their informed consent.

SLAVERY, SERVITUDE AND FORCED LABOUR

13. No one may be subjected to slavery, servitude or forced labour.

PRIVACY

14. Everyone has the right to privacy, which includes the right not to have —

(a) their person or home searched;

(b) their property searched;

(c) their possessions seized; or

(d) the privacy of their communications infringed.

FREEDOM OF RELIGION, BELIEF AND OPINION

15. (1)   Everyone has the right to freedom of conscience, religion, thought, belief and opinion.

(2)   Religious observances may be conducted at state or state-aided institutions, provided that —

(a) those observances follow rules made by the appropriate public authorities;

(b) they are conducted on an equitable basis; and

(c) attendance at them is free and voluntary.

(3)   (a) This section does not prevent legislation recognising —

i. marriages concluded under any tradition, or a system of religious, personal or family law; or

ii. systems of personal and family law under any tradition, or adhered to by persons professing a particular religion.

(b) Recognition in terms of paragraph (a) must be consistent with this section and the other provisions of the Constitution.

FREEDOM OF EXPRESSION

16. (1)   Everyone has the right to freedom of expression, which includes —

(a) freedom of the press and other media;

(b) freedom to receive or impart information or ideas;

(c) freedom of artistic creativity; and

(d) academic freedom and freedom of scientific research.

(2)   The right in subsection (1) does not extend to —

(a) propaganda for war;

(b) incitement of imminent violence; or

(c) advocacy of hatred that is based on race, ethnicity, gender or religion, and that constitutes incitement to cause harm.

ASSEMBLY, DEMONSTRATION, PICKET AND PETITION

17. Everyone has the right, peacefully and unarmed, to assemble, to demonstrate, to picket and to present petitions.

FREEDOM OF ASSOCIATION

18. Everyone has the right to freedom of association.

POLITICAL RIGHTS

19. (1)   Every citizen is free to make political choices, which includes the right —

(a) to form a political party;

(b) to participate in the activities of, or recruit members for, a political party; and

(c) to campaign for a political party or cause.

(2)   Every citizen has the right to free, fair and regular elections for any legislative body established in terms of the Constitution.

(3)   Every adult citizen has the right —

(a) to vote in elections for any legislative body established in terms of the Constitution, and to do so in secret; and

(b) to stand for public office and, if elected, to hold office.

CITIZENSHIP

20. No citizen may be deprived of citizenship.

FREEDOM OF MOVEMENT AND RESIDENCE

21. (1) Everyone has the right to freedom of movement.
(2) Everyone has the right to leave the Republic.
(3) Every citizen has the right to enter, to remain in and to reside anywhere in, the Republic.
(4) Every citizen has the right to a passport.

FREEDOM OF TRADE, OCCUPATION AND PROFESSION

22. Every citizen has the right to choose their trade, occupation or profession freely. The practice of a trade, occupation or profession may be regulated by law.

LABOUR RELATIONS

23. (1) Everyone has the right to fair labour practices.
(2) Every worker has the right —
(a) to form and join a trade union;
(b) to participate in the activities and programmes of a trade union; and
(c) to strike.
(3) Every employer has the right —
(a) to form and join an employers' organisation; and
(b) to participate in the activities and programmes of an employers' organisation.
(4) Every trade union and every employers' organisation has the right —
(a) to determine its own administration, programmes and activities;
(b) to organise; and
(c) to form and join a federation.
(5) Every trade union, employers' organisation and employer has the right to engage in collective bargaining. National legislation may be enacted to regulate collective bargaining. To the extent that the legislation may limit a right in this Chapter, the limitation must comply with section 36(1).
(6) National legislation may recognise union security arrangements contained in collective agreements. To the extent that the legislation may limit a right in this Chapter, the limitation must comply with section 36(1).

ENVIRONMENT

24. Everyone has the right —
(a) to an environment that is not harmful to their health or well-being; and
(b) to have the environment protected, for the benefit of present and future generations, through reasonable legislative and other measures that —
i. prevent pollution and ecological degradation;
ii. promote conservation; and
iii. secure ecologically sustainable development and use of natural resources while promoting justifiable economic and social development.

PROPERTY

25. (1)   No one may be deprived of property except in terms of law of general application, and no law may permit arbitrary deprivation of property.

(2)   Property may be expropriated only in terms of law of general application —
(a) for a public purpose or in the public interest; and
(b) subject to compensation, the amount of which and the time and manner of payment of which have either been agreed to by those affected or decided or approved by a court.

(3)   The amount of the compensation and the time and manner of payment must be just and equitable, reflecting an equitable balance between the public interest and the interests of those affected, having regard to all relevant circumstances, including —
(a) the current use of the property;
(b) the history of the acquisition and use of the property;
(c) the market value of the property;
(d) the extent of direct state investment and subsidy in the acquisition and beneficial capital improvement of the property; and
(e) the purpose of the expropriation.

(4)   For the purposes of this section —
(a) the public interest includes the nation's commitment to land reform, and to reforms to bring about equitable access to all South Africa's natural resources; and
(b) property is not limited to land.

(5)   The state must take reasonable legislative and other measures, within its available resources, to foster conditions which enable citizens to gain access to land on an equitable basis.

(6)   A person or community whose tenure of land is legally insecure as a result of past racially discriminatory laws or practices is entitled, to the extent provided by an Act of Parliament, either to tenure which is legally secure or to comparable redress.

(7)   A person or community dispossessed of property after 19 June 1913 as a result of past racially discriminatory laws or practices is entitled, to the extent provided by an Act of Parliament, either to restitution of that property or to equitable redress.

(8)   No provision of this section may impede the state from taking legislative and other measures to achieve land, water and related reform, in order to redress the results of past racial discrimination, provided that any departure from the provisions of this section is in accordance with the provisions of section 36(1).

(9)   Parliament must enact the legislation referred to in subsection (6).

HOUSING

26. (1)   Everyone has the right to have access to adequate housing.

(2)   The state must take reasonable legislative and other measures, within its available resources, to achieve the progressive realisation of this right.

(3)   No one may be evicted from their home, or have their home demolished, without an order of court made after considering all the relevant circumstances. No legislation may permit arbitrary evictions.

HEALTH CARE, FOOD, WATER AND SOCIAL SECURITY

27. (1) Everyone has the right to have access to —
    (a) health care services, including reproductive health care;
    (b) sufficient food and water; and
    (c) social security, including, if they are unable to support themselves and their dependants, appropriate social assistance.
    (2) The state must take reasonable legislative and other measures, within its available resources, to achieve the progressive realisation of each of these rights.
    (3) No one may be refused emergency medical treatment.

CHILDREN

28. (1) Every child has the right —
    (a) to a name and a nationality from birth;
    (b) to family care or parental care, or to appropriate alternative care when removed from the family environment;
    (c) to basic nutrition, shelter, basic health care services and social services;
    (d) to be protected from maltreatment, neglect, abuse or degradation;
    (e) to be protected from exploitative labour practices;
    (f) not to be required or permitted to perform work or provide services that —
        i. are inappropriate for a person of that child's age; or
        ii. place at risk the child's well-being, education, physical or mental health or spiritual, moral or social development;
    (g) not to be detained except as a measure of last resort, in which case, in addition to the rights a child enjoys under sections 12 and 35, the child may be detained only for the shortest appropriate period of time, and has the right to be —
        i. kept separately from detained persons over the age of 18 years; and
        ii. treated in a manner, and kept in conditions, that take account of the child's age;
    (h) to have a legal practitioner assigned to the child by the state, and at state expense, in civil proceedings affecting the child, if substantial injustice would otherwise result; and
    (i) not to be used directly in armed conflict, and to be protected in times of armed conflict.
    (2) A child's best interests are of paramount importance in every matter concerning the child.
    (3) In this section 'child' means a person under the age of 18 years.

EDUCATION

29. (1) Everyone has the right —
    (a) to a basic education, including adult basic education; and
    (b) to further education, which the state, through reasonable measures, must make progressively available and accessible.
    (2) Everyone has the right to receive education in the official language or languages of their choice in public educational institutions where that education is reasonably practicable. In order to ensure the effective access to, and implementation of, this right, the state must consider all reasonable educational alternatives, including single medium institutions, taking into account —

(a) equity;

(b) practicability; and

(c) the need to redress the results of past racially discriminatory laws and practices.

(3)   Everyone has the right to establish and maintain, at their own expense, independent educational institutions that —

(a) do not discriminate on the basis of race;

(b) are registered with the state; and

(c) maintain standards that are not inferior to standards at comparable public educational institutions.

(4)   Subsection (3) does not preclude state subsidies for independent educational institutions.

LANGUAGE AND CULTURE

30.   Everyone has the right to use the language and to participate in the cultural life of their choice, but no one exercising these rights may do so in a manner inconsistent with any provision of the Bill of Rights.

CULTURAL, RELIGIOUS AND LINGUISTIC COMMUNITIES

31.   (1)   Persons belonging to a cultural, religious or linguistic community may not be denied the right, with other members of that community —

(a) to enjoy their culture, practise their religion and use their language; and

(b) to form, join and maintain cultural, religious and linguistic associations and other organs of civil society.

(2)   The rights in subsection (1) may not be exercised in a manner inconsistent with any provision of the Bill of Rights.

ACCESS TO INFORMATION

32.   (1)   Everyone has the right of access to —

(a) any information held by the state; and

(b) any information that is held by another person and that is required for the exercise or protection of any rights.

(2)   National legislation must be enacted to give effect to this right, and may provide for reasonable measures to alleviate the administrative and financial burden on the state.

JUST ADMINISTRATIVE ACTION

33.   (1)   Everyone has the right to administrative action that is lawful, reasonable and procedurally fair.

(2)   Everyone whose rights have been adversely affected by administrative action has the right to be given written reasons.

(3)   National legislation must be enacted to give effect to these rights, and must —

(a) provide for the review of administrative action by a court or, where appropriate, an independent and impartial tribunal;

(b) impose a duty on the state to give effect to the rights in subsections (1) and (2); and

(c) promote an efficient administration.

ACCESS TO COURTS

34. Everyone has the right to have any dispute that can be resolved by the application of law decided in a fair public hearing before a court or, where appropriate, another independent and impartial tribunal or forum.

ARRESTED, DETAINED AND ACCUSED PERSONS

35. (1) Everyone who is arrested for allegedly committing an offence has the right —
    (a) to remain silent;
    (b) to be informed promptly —
        i. of the right to remain silent; and
        ii. of the consequences of not remaining silent;
    (c) not to be compelled to make any confession or admission that could be used in evidence against that person;
    (d) to be brought before a court as soon as reasonably possible, but not later than —
        i. 48 hours after the arrest; or
        ii. the end of the first court day after the expiry of the 48 hours, if the 48 hours expire outside ordinary court hours or on a day which is not an ordinary court day;
    (e) at the first court appearance after being arrested, to be charged or to be informed of the reason for the detention to continue, or to be released; and
    (f) to be released from detention if the interests of justice permit, subject to reasonable conditions.

    (2) Everyone who is detained, including every sentenced prisoner, has the right —
    (a) to be informed promptly of the reason for being detained;
    (b) to choose, and to consult with, a legal practitioner, and to be informed of this right promptly;
    (c) to have a legal practitioner assigned to the detained person by the state and at state expense, if substantial injustice would otherwise result, and to be informed of this right promptly;
    (d) to challenge the lawfulness of the detention in person before a court and, if the detention is unlawful, to be released;
    (e) to conditions of detention that are consistent with human dignity, including at least exercise and the provision, at state expense, of adequate accommodation, nutrition, reading material and medical treatment; and
    (f) to communicate with, and be visited by, that person's —
        i. spouse or partner;
        ii. next of kin;
        iii. chosen religious counsellor; and
        iv. chosen medical practitioner.

    (3) Every accused person has a right to a fair trial, which includes the right —
    (a) to be informed of the charge with sufficient detail to answer it;
    (b) to have adequate time and facilities to prepare a defence;
    (c) to a public trial before an ordinary court;
    (d) to have their trial begin and conclude without unreasonable delay;
    (e) to be present when being tried;
    (f) to choose, and be represented by, a legal practitioner, and to be informed of this right promptly;

(g) to have a legal practitioner assigned to the accused person by the state and at state expense, if substantial injustice would otherwise result, and to be informed of this right promptly;

(h) to be presumed innocent, to remain silent, and not to testify during the proceedings;

(i) to adduce and challenge evidence;

(j) not to be compelled to give self-incriminating evidence;

(k) to be tried in a language that the accused person understands or, if that is not practicable, to have the proceedings interpreted in that language;

(l) not to be convicted for an act or omission that was not an offence under either national or international law at the time it was committed or omitted;

(m) not to be tried for an offence in respect of an act or omission for which that person has previously been either acquitted or convicted;

(n) to the benefit of the least severe of the prescribed punishments if the prescribed punishment for the offence has been changed between the time that the offence was committed and the time of sentencing; and

(o) of appeal to, or review by, a higher court.

(4) Whenever this section requires information to be given to a person, that information must be given in a language that the person understands.

(5) Evidence obtained in a manner that violates any right in the Bill of Rights must be excluded if the admission of that evidence would render the trial unfair or otherwise be detrimental to the administration of justice.

LIMITATION OF RIGHTS

36. (1) The rights in the Bill of Rights may be limited only in terms of law of general application to the extent that the limitation is reasonable and justifiable in an open and democratic society based on human dignity, equality and freedom, taking into account all relevant factors, including —

(a) the nature of the right;

(b) the importance of the purpose of the limitation;

(c) the nature and extent of the limitation;

(d) the relation between the limitation and its purpose; and

(e) less restrictive means to achieve the purpose.

(2) Except as provided in subsection (1) or in any other provision of the Constitution, no law may limit any right entrenched in the Bill of Rights.

STATES OF EMERGENCY

37. (1) A state of emergency may be declared only in terms of an Act of Parliament, and only when —

(a) the life of the nation is threatened by war, invasion, general insurrection, disorder, natural disaster or other public emergency; and

(b) the declaration is necessary to restore peace and order.

(2) A declaration of a state of emergency, and any legislation enacted or other action taken in consequence of that declaration, may be effective only —

(a) prospectively; and

(b) for no more than 21 days from the date of the declaration, unless the National Assembly resolves to extend the declaration. The Assembly may extend a declaration of a state of emergency for no more than three months at a time. The first extension of the state of emergency must be by a resolution adopted with a supporting vote of a majority of the members of the Assembly. Any subsequent extension must be by a resolution adopted with a supporting vote of at least 60 per cent of the members of the Assembly. A resolution in terms of this paragraph may be adopted only following a public debate in the Assembly.

(3) Any competent court may decide on the validity of —
(a) a declaration of a state of emergency;
(b) any extension of a declaration of a state of emergency; or
(c) any legislation enacted, or other action taken, in consequence of a declaration of a state of emergency.

(4) Any legislation enacted in consequence of a declaration of a state of emergency may derogate from the Bill of Rights only to the extent that —
(a) the derogation is strictly required by the emergency; and
(b) the legislation —
i. is consistent with the Republic's obligations under international law applicable to states of emergency;
ii. conforms to subsection (5); and
iii. is published in the national Government Gazette as soon as reasonably possible after being enacted.

(5) No Act of Parliament that authorises a declaration of a state of emergency, and no legislation enacted or other action taken in consequence of a declaration, may permit or authorise —
(a) indemnifying the state, or any person, in respect of any unlawful act;
(b) any derogation from this section; or
(c) any derogation from a section mentioned in column 1 of the Table of Non-Derogable Rights, to the extent indicated opposite that section in column 3 of the Table.

TABLE OF NON-DEROGABLE RIGHTS

1 Section Number	2 Section Title	3 Extent to which the right is protected
9	Equality	With respect to unfair discrimination solely on the grounds of race, colour, ethnic or social origin, sex, religion or language
10	Human Dignity	Entirely
11	Life	Entirely
12	Freedom and Security of the person	With respect to subsections (1)(d) and (e) and (2)(c)
13	Slavery, servitude and forced labour	With respect to slavery and servitude
28	Children	With respect to: • subsection (1)(d) and (e); • the rights in subparagraphs (i) and (ii) of subsection (1)(g); and • subsection 1(i) in respect of children of 15 years and younger
35	Arrested, detained and accused persons	With respect to: • subsections (1)(a), (b) and(c) and (2)(d); • the rights in paragraphs (a) to (o) of subsection (3), excluding paragraph (d) • subsection (4); and • subsection (5) with respect to the exclusion of evidence if the admission of that evidence would render the trial unfair.

(6) Whenever anyone is detained without trial in consequence of a derogation of rights resulting from a declaration of a state of emergency, the following conditions must be observed:

(a) An adult family member or friend of the detainee must be contacted as soon as reasonably possible, and informed that the person has been detained.

(b) A notice must be published in the national Government Gazette within five days of the person being detained, stating the detainee's name and place of detention and referring to the emergency measure in terms of which that person has been detained.

(c) The detainee must be allowed to choose, and be visited at any reasonable time by, a medical practitioner.

(d) The detainee must be allowed to choose, and be visited at any reasonable time by, a legal representative.

(e) A court must review the detention as soon as reasonably possible, but no later than 10 days after the date the person was detained, and the court must release the detainee unless it is necessary to continue the detention to restore peace and order.

(f) A detainee who is not released in terms of a review under paragraph (e), or who is not released in terms of a review under this paragraph, may apply to a court for a further review of the detention at any time after 10 days have passed since the previous review, and the court must release the detainee unless it is still necessary to continue the detention to restore peace and order.

(g) The detainee must be allowed to appear in person before any court considering the detention, to be represented by a legal practitioner at those hearings, and to make representations against continued detention.

(h) The state must present written reasons to the court to justify the continued detention of the detainee, and must give a copy of those reasons to the detainee at least two days before the court reviews the detention.

(7) If a court releases a detainee, that person may not be detained again on the same grounds unless the state first shows a court good cause for re-detaining that person.

(8) Subsections (6) and (7) do not apply to persons who are not South African citizens and who are detained in consequence of an international armed conflict. Instead, the state must comply with the standards binding on the Republic under international humanitarian law in respect of the detention of such persons.

ENFORCEMENT OF RIGHTS

38. Anyone listed in this section has the right to approach a competent court, alleging that a right in the Bill of Rights has been infringed or threatened, and the court may grant appropriate relief, including a declaration of rights. The persons who may approach a court are —

(a) anyone acting in their own interest;

(b) anyone acting on behalf of another person who cannot act in their own name;

(c) anyone acting as a member of, or in the interest of, a group or class of persons;

(d) anyone acting in the public interest; and

(e) an association acting in the interest of its members.

INTERPRETATION OF BILL OF RIGHTS

39. (1)   When interpreting the Bill of Rights, a court, tribunal or forum —
       (a) must promote the values that underlie an open and democratic society based on human dignity, equality and freedom;
       (b) must consider international law; and
       (c) may consider foreign law.
    (2)   When interpreting any legislation, and when developing the common law or customary law, every court, tribunal or forum must promote the spirit, purport and objects of the Bill of Rights.
    (3)   The Bill of Rights does not deny the existence of any other rights or freedoms that are recognised or conferred by common law, customary law or legislation, to the extent that they are consistent with the Bill.

SOURCE South African Constitution 1996, Bill of Rights
http://www.polity.org.za/govdocs/constitution/saconst02.html

APPENDIX D

UNITED KINGDOM HUMAN RIGHTS ACT 1998

INTRODUCTION

1. (1) In this Act 'the Convention rights' means the rights and fundamental freedoms set out in —

    (a) Articles 2 to 12 and 14 of the [European] Convention [for the Protection of Human Rights and Fundamental Freedoms signed at Rome on 4 November 1950]

    (b) Articles 1 to 3 of the First Protocol [to the Convention], and

    (c) Articles 1 and 2 of the Sixth Protocol [to the Convention], as read with Articles 16 to 18 of the Convention.

    (2)   Those Articles are to have effect for the purposes of this Act subject to any designated derogation or reservation ...

    (3)   The Articles are set out in Schedule 1 ...

INTERPRETATION OF CONVENTION RIGHTS

2. (1)   A court or tribunal determining a question which has arisen in connection with a Convention right must take into account any —

    (a) judgment, decision, declaration or advisory opinion of the European Court of Human Rights,

    (b) opinion of the Commission given in a report adopted under Article 31 of the Convention,

    (c) decision of the Commission in connection with Article 26 or 27(2) of the Convention, or

    (d) decision of the Committee of Ministers taken under Article 46 of the Convention,

    whenever made or given, so far as, in the opinion of the court or tribunal, it is relevant to the proceedings in which that question has arisen.

LEGISLATION

3. (1) So far as it is possible to do so, primary legislation and subordinate legislation must be read and given effect in a way which is compatible with the Convention rights.
    (2) This section —
    (a) applies to primary legislation and subordinate legislation whenever enacted;
    (b) does not affect the validity, continuing operation or enforcement of any incompatible primary legislation; and
    (c) does not affect the validity, continuing operation or enforcement of any incompatible subordinate legislation if (disregarding any possibility of revocation) primary legislation prevents removal of the incompatibility.

4. (1) Subsection (2) applies in any proceedings in which a court determines whether a provision of primary legislation is compatible with a Convention right.
    (2) If the court is satisfied that the provision is incompatible with a Convention right, it may make a declaration of that incompatibility.
    (3) Subsection (4) applies in any proceedings in which a court determines whether a provision of subordinate legislation, made in the exercise of a power conferred by primary legislation, is compatible with a Convention right.
    (4) If the court is satisfied —
    (a) that the provision is incompatible with a Convention right, and
    (b) that (disregarding any possibility of revocation) the primary legislation concerned prevents removal of the incompatibility,
    it may make a declaration of that incompatibility ...
    (6) A declaration under this section ('a declaration of incompatibility') —
    (a) does not affect the validity, continuing operation or enforcement of the provision in respect of which it is given; and
    (b) is not binding on the parties to the proceedings in which it is made ...

PUBLIC AUTHORITIES

6. (1) It is unlawful for a public authority to act in a way which is incompatible with a Convention right.
    (2) Subsection (1) does not apply to an act if —
    (a) as the result of one or more provisions of primary legislation, the authority could not have acted differently; or
    (b) in the case of one or more provisions of, or made under, primary legislation which cannot be read or given effect in a way which is compatible with the Convention rights, the authority was acting so as to give effect to or enforce those provisions.
    (3) In this section 'public authority' includes —
    (a) a court or tribunal, and
    (b) any person certain of whose functions are functions of a public nature,
    but does not include either House of Parliament or a person exercising functions in connection with proceedings in Parliament.

7. (1) A person who claims that a public authority has acted (or proposes to act) in a way which is made unlawful by section 6(1) may —

(a) bring proceedings against the authority under this Act in the appropriate court or tribunal, or

(b) rely on the Convention right or rights concerned in any legal proceedings,

but only if he is (or would be) a victim of the unlawful act ...

8. (1)   In relation to any act (or proposed act) of a public authority which the court finds is (or would be) unlawful, it may grant such relief or remedy, or make such order, within its powers as it considers just and appropriate ...

(2)   But damages may be awarded only by a court which has power to award damages, or to order the payment of compensation, in civil proceedings.

REMEDIAL ACTION

10. (1)   This section applies if —

(a) a provision of legislation has been declared under section 4 to be incompatible with a Convention right and, if an appeal lies —

i. all persons who may appeal have stated in writing that they do not intend to do so;

ii. the time for bringing an appeal has expired and no appeal has been brought within that time; or

iii. an appeal brought within that time has been determined or abandoned; or

(b) it appears to a Minister of the Crown or Her Majesty in Council that, having regard to a finding of the European Court of Human Rights made after the coming into force of this section in proceedings against the United Kingdom, a provision of legislation is incompatible with an obligation of the United Kingdom arising from the Convention.

(2) If a Minister of the Crown considers that there are compelling reasons for proceeding under this section, he may by order make such amendments to the legislation as he considers necessary to remove the incompatibility.

(3) If, in the case of subordinate legislation, a Minister of the Crown considers —

(a) that it is necessary to amend the primary legislation under which the subordinate legislation in question was made, in order to enable the incompatibility to be removed, and

(b) that there are compelling reasons for proceeding under this section,

he may by order make such amendments to the primary legislation as he considers necessary.

PARLIAMENTARY PROCEDURE

19. (1)   A Minister of the Crown in charge of a Bill in either House of Parliament must, before Second Reading of the Bill —

(a) make a statement to the effect that in his view the provisions of the Bill are compatible with the Convention rights ('a statement of compatibility'); or

(b) make a statement to the effect that although he is unable to make a statement of compatibility the government nevertheless wishes the House to proceed with the Bill.

SCHEDULE I — THE ARTICLES
PART I
THE EUROPEAN CONVENTION FOR THE PROTECTION OF HUMAN RIGHTS AND FUNDAMENTAL FREEDOMS SIGNED AT ROME ON 4 NOVEMBER 1950

ARTICLE 2
RIGHT TO LIFE

1. Everyone's right to life shall be protected by law. No one shall be deprived of his life intentionally save in the execution of a sentence of a court following his conviction of a crime for which this penalty is provided by law.

2. Deprivation of life shall not be regarded as inflicted in contravention of this Article when it results from the use of force which is no more than absolutely necessary:

(a) in defence of any person from unlawful violence;

(b) in order to effect a lawful arrest or to prevent the escape of a person lawfully detained;

(c) in action lawfully taken for the purpose of quelling a riot or insurrection.

ARTICLE 3
PROHIBITION OF TORTURE

No one shall be subjected to torture or to inhuman or degrading treatment or punishment.

ARTICLE 4
PROHIBITION OF SLAVERY AND FORCED LABOUR

1. No one shall be held in slavery or servitude.

2. No one shall be required to perform forced or compulsory labour.

3. For the purpose of this Article the term 'forced or compulsory labour' shall not include:

(a) any work required to be done in the ordinary course of detention imposed according to the provisions of Article 5 of this Convention or during conditional release from such detention;

(b) any service of a military character or, in case of conscientious objectors in countries where they are recognised, service exacted instead of compulsory military service;

(c) any service exacted in case of an emergency or calamity threatening the life or well-being of the community;

(d) any work or service which forms part of normal civic obligations.

ARTICLE 5
RIGHT TO LIBERTY AND SECURITY

1. Everyone has the right to liberty and security of person. No one shall be deprived of his liberty save in the following cases and in accordance with a procedure prescribed by law:

(a) the lawful detention of a person after conviction by a competent court;

(b) the lawful arrest or detention of a person for non-compliance with the lawful order of a court or in order to secure the fulfilment of any obligation prescribed by law;

(c) the lawful arrest or detention of a person effected for the purpose of bringing him before the competent legal authority on reasonable suspicion of having committed an offence or when it is reasonably considered necessary to prevent his committing an offence or fleeing after having done so;

(d) the detention of a minor by lawful order for the purpose of educational supervision or his lawful detention for the purpose of bringing him before the competent legal authority;

(e) the lawful detention of persons for the prevention of the spreading of infectious diseases, of persons of unsound mind, alcoholics or drug addicts or vagrants;

(f) the lawful arrest or detention of a person to prevent his effecting an unauthorised entry into the country or of a person against whom action is being taken with a view to deportation or extradition.

2. Everyone who is arrested shall be informed promptly, in a language which he understands, of the reasons for his arrest and of any charge against him.

3. Everyone arrested or detained in accordance with the provisions of paragraph 1(c) of this Article shall be brought promptly before a judge or other officer authorised by law to exercise judicial power and shall be entitled to trial within a reasonable time or to release pending trial. Release may be conditioned by guarantees to appear for trial.

4. Everyone who is deprived of his liberty by arrest or detention shall be entitled to take proceedings by which the lawfulness of his detention shall be decided speedily by a court and his release ordered if the detention is not lawful.

5. Everyone who has been the victim of arrest or detention in contravention of the provisions of this Article shall have an enforceable right to compensation.

ARTICLE 6
RIGHT TO A FAIR TRIAL

1. In the determination of his civil rights and obligations or of any criminal charge against him, everyone is entitled to a fair and public hearing within a reasonable time by an independent and impartial tribunal established by law. Judgment shall be pronounced publicly but the press and public may be excluded from all or part of the trial in the interest of morals, public order or national security in a democratic society, where the interests of juveniles or the protection of the private life of the parties so require, or to the extent strictly necessary in the opinion of the court in special circumstances where publicity would prejudice the interests of justice.

2. Everyone charged with a criminal offence shall be presumed innocent until proved guilty according to law.

3. Everyone charged with a criminal offence has the following minimum rights:

(a) to be informed promptly, in a language which he understands and in detail, of the nature and cause of the accusation against him;

(b) to have adequate time and facilities for the preparation of his defence;

(c) to defend himself in person or through legal assistance of his own choosing or, if he has not sufficient means to pay for legal assistance, to be given it free when the interests of justice so require;

(d) to examine or have examined witnesses against him and to obtain the attendance and examination of witnesses on his behalf under the same con-

ditions as witnesses against him;
(e) to have the free assistance of an interpreter if he cannot understand or speak the language used in court.

ARTICLE 7
NO PUNISHMENT WITHOUT LAW

1. No one shall be held guilty of any criminal offence on account of any act or omission which did not constitute a criminal offence under national or international law at the time when it was committed. Nor shall a heavier penalty be imposed than the one that was applicable at the time the criminal offence was committed.

2. This Article shall not prejudice the trial and punishment of any person for any act or omission which, at the time when it was committed, was criminal according to the general principles of law recognised by civilised nations.

ARTICLE 8
RIGHT TO RESPECT FOR PRIVATE AND FAMILY LIFE

1. Everyone has the right to respect for his private and family life, his home and his correspondence.

2. There shall be no interference by a public authority with the exercise of this right except such as is in accordance with the law and is necessary in a democratic society in the interests of national security, public safety or the economic well-being of the country, for the prevention of disorder or crime, for the protection of health or morals, or for the protection of the rights and freedoms of others.

ARTICLE 9
FREEDOM OF THOUGHT, CONSCIENCE AND RELIGION

1. Everyone has the right to freedom of thought, conscience and religion; this right includes freedom to change his religion or belief and freedom, either alone or in community with others and in public or private, to manifest his religion or belief, in worship, teaching, practice and observance.

2. Freedom to manifest one's religion or beliefs shall be subject only to such limitations as are prescribed by law and are necessary in a democratic society in the interests of public safety, for the protection of public order, health or morals, or for the protection of the rights and freedoms of others.

ARTICLE 10
FREEDOM OF EXPRESSION

1. Everyone has the right to freedom of expression. This right shall include freedom to hold opinions and to receive and impart information and ideas without interference by public authority and regardless of frontiers. This Article shall not prevent States from requiring the licensing of broadcasting, television or cinema enterprises.

2. The exercise of these freedoms, since it carries with it duties and responsibilities, may be subject to such formalities, conditions, restrictions or penalties as are prescribed by law and are necessary in a democratic society, in the interests of national security, territorial integrity or public safety, for the prevention of disorder or crime, for the protection of health or morals, for the protection of the reputation or rights of others, for preventing the disclosure of information received in confidence, or for maintaining the authority and impartiality of the judiciary.

ARTICLE 11
FREEDOM OF ASSEMBLY AND ASSOCIATION

1. Everyone has the right to freedom of peaceful assembly and to freedom of association with others, including the right to form and to join trade unions for the protection of his interests.

2. No restrictions shall be placed on the exercise of these rights other than such as are prescribed by law and are necessary in a democratic society in the interests of national security or public safety, for the prevention of disorder or crime, for the protection of health or morals or for the protection of the rights and freedoms of others. This Article shall not prevent the imposition of lawful restrictions on the exercise of these rights by members of the armed forces, of the police or of the administration of the State.

ARTICLE 12
RIGHT TO MARRY

Men and women of marriageable age have the right to marry and to found a family, according to the national laws governing the exercise of this right.

ARTICLE 14
PROHIBITION OF DISCRIMINATION

The enjoyment of the rights and freedoms set forth in this Convention shall be secured without discrimination on any ground such as sex, race, colour, language, religion, political or other opinion, national or social origin, association with a national minority, property, birth or other status.

ARTICLE 16
RESTRICTIONS ON POLITICAL ACTIVITY OF ALIENS

Nothing in Articles 10, 11 and 14 shall be regarded as preventing the High Contracting Parties from imposing restrictions on the political activity of aliens.

ARTICLE 17
PROHIBITION OF ABUSE OF RIGHTS

Nothing in this Convention may be interpreted as implying for any State, group or person any right to engage in any activity or perform any act aimed at the destruction of any of the rights and freedoms set forth herein or at their limitation to a greater extent than is provided for in the Convention.

ARTICLE 18
LIMITATION ON USE OF RESTRICTIONS ON RIGHTS

The restrictions permitted under this Convention to the said rights and freedoms shall not be applied for any purpose other than those for which they have been prescribed.

SCHEDULE I,
PART II
FIRST PROTOCOL

ARTICLE I
PROTECTION OF PROPERTY

Every natural or legal person is entitled to the peaceful enjoyment of his possessions. No one shall be deprived of his possessions except in the public interest and subject to the conditions provided for by law and by the general principles of international law. The preceding provisions shall not, however, in any way impair the right of a State to enforce such laws as it deems necessary to control the use of property in accordance with the general interest or to secure the payment of taxes or other contributions or penalties.

ARTICLE 2
RIGHT TO EDUCATION

No person shall be denied the right to education. In the exercise of any functions which it assumes in relation to education and to teaching, the State shall respect the right of parents to ensure such education and teaching in conformity with their own religious and philosophical convictions.

ARTICLE 3
RIGHT TO FREE ELECTIONS

The High Contracting Parties undertake to hold free elections at reasonable intervals by secret ballot, under conditions which will ensure the free expression of the opinion of the people in the choice of the legislature.

SCHEDULE I, PART III
SIXTH PROTOCOL

ARTICLE I
ABOLITION OF THE DEATH PENALTY

The death penalty shall be abolished. No one shall be condemned to such penalty or executed.

ARTICLE 2
DEATH PENALTY IN TIME OF WAR

A State may make provision in its law for the death penalty in respect of acts committed in time of war or of imminent threat of war; such penalty shall be applied only in the instances laid down in the law and in accordance with its provisions. The State shall communicate to the Secretary General of the Council of Europe the relevant provisions of that law.

SOURCE United Kingdom Human Rights Act 1998
http://www.hmso.gov.uk/acts/acts1998/19980042.htm

NOTES

INTRODUCTION

1   Frank Kermode, *The Sense of an Ending*, Oxford University Press, New York, 1967, p 11.

CHAPTER 1 A CONSTITUTIONAL SILENCE

1   See the discussion in Murray Gleeson, *The Rule of Law and the Constitution*, ABC Books, Sydney, 2000, pp 67–68.

2   Andrew Inglis Clark, *Studies in Australian Constitutional Law*, Maxwell, Melbourne, 1901, p 358.

3   For example, Charles Black, *Structure and Relationship in Constitutional Law*, Louisiana State University Press, Baton Rouge, 1969, p 25.

4   Zelman Cowan, 'A Comparison of the Constitutions of Australia and the United States', 4 *Buffalo Law Review* (1955) 155, pp 165–68.

5   RCL Moffatt, 'Philosophical Foundations of the Australian Constitutional Tradition', 5 *Sydney Law Review* (1965) 59, pp 85–88.

6   James Bryce, *Studies in History and Jurisprudence*, vol. I, Clarendon Press, Oxford, 1901, pp 502–503, 538.

7   In 1891 in Sydney; in 1897–8 in Adelaide, Sydney and Melbourne.

8   Alfred Deakin, *The Federal Story: The Inner Story of the Federal Cause*, Robertson & Mullens, Melbourne, 1944, p 30.

9   Andrew Inglis Clark, *Studies in Australian Constitutional Law*, pp 386–87.

10 For example, *Schenck v US* 249 US 47 (1919), *Abrams v US* 250 US 616 (1919).

11 *Reynolds v Clark* 98 US 145 (1878).

12 For example, *Yick Wo v Hopkins* 118 US 356 (1886), *Strauder v West Virginia* 100 US 303 (1880).

13 *Official Record of the Debates of the Australasian Federal Convention, Third Session, Melbourne, 20 January to 17 March 1898*, RS Brain, Government Printer,

Melbourne (*Melbourne Debates 1898*), p 1770.

14 *Melbourne Debates 1898*, p 660.

15 *Melbourne Debates 1898*, p 1770.

16 *Official Record of the Debates of the Australasian Federal Convention Second Session, Sydney, 2 to 24 September 1897*, WA Gullick, Government Printer, Sydney (*Sydney Proceedings 1897*) p 149.

17 *An Australian Handbook of Federal Government*, Angus & Robertson, Sydney,1897, p 173.

18 *Melbourne Debates 1898*, p 666.

19 *Yick Wo v Hopkins* 118 US 356 (1886).

20 *Melbourne Debates 1898*, p 687.

21 *Melbourne Debates 1898*, pp 685–86.

22 *Melbourne Debates 1898*, p 1801.

23 *Melbourne Debates 1898*, p 688.

24 Quoted in Helen Irving, *To Constitute a Nation: A Cultural History of Australia's Constitution*, Cambridge University Press, Melbourne, 1997, p 103. For a discussion of the way anti-Chinese feeling was manifested in constitutional drafters' discussion of citizenship see Kim Rubenstein, 'Citizenship and the Constitutional Convention Debates: A Mere Legal Inference?', 25 *Federal Law Review* (1997) 295.

25 *Melbourne Debates 1898*, p 688.

26 Helen Irving, *To Constitute a Nation*, pp 100–118.

27 Murray Gleeson, *The Rule of Law and the Constitution*, pp 26–27.

28 Helen Irving, *To Constitute a Nation*, pp 101–102.

29 *The Canberra Times*, 19 February 2000, p 1.

30 *Cheatle v The Queen* (1993) 177 CLR 541.

31 *R v Archdall and Roskruge* (1928) 41 CLR 128.

32 *Spratt v Hermes* (1965) 114 CLR 226, 244.

33 (2000) 175 ALR 338.

34 See Amelia Simpson & Mary Wood, '"A Puny Thing Indeed" — *Cheng v The Queen* and the Constitutional Right to Trial by Jury', 29 *Federal Law Review* (2001) 95, pp 107–110.

35 (2000) 175 ALR 338 paragraph 218.

36 See *Church of the New Faith v Commissioner of Pay-Roll Tax (Vic)* (1983) 154 CLR 120. For an analysis of the case see Bruce Kaye, 'An Australian definition of religion', 14 *University of New South Wales Law Journal* (1991) 332.

37 *Attorney-General (Vic); ex rel Black v Commonwealth* (1981) 146 CLR 321.

38 (1981) 146 CLR 321 p 609 (Stephen J). See also p 603 (Gibbs J).

39 (1981) 146 CLR 321 pp 652–53 (Wilson J).

40 (1912) 15 CLR 366.

41 (1912) 15 CLR 366, pp 371, 369.

42 (1912) 15 CLR 366, p 373.

43 *Adelaide Company of Jehovah's Witnesses Incorporated v Commonwealth* (1943) 67 CLR 116, p 131.

44 67 CLR 116, p 149.

45 (1997) 190 CLR 1.

46 (1997) 190 CLR 1, pp 131–32.

47 For example, *Henry v Boehm* (1973) 128 CLR 482.

48 (1989) 168 CLR 461.

49 *Nationwide News Pty Ltd v Wills* (1992) 177 CLR 1; *Australian Capital Television Pty Ltd v Commonwealth* (1992) 177 CLR 106.

50 *Theophanous v Herald & Weekly Times Ltd* (1994) 182 CLR 104; *Stephens v Western Australian Newspapers Ltd* (1994) 182 CLR 211.

51 *Lange v Australian Broadcasting Commission* (1997) 189 CLR 520. For a critique of the High Court's jurisprudence in this series of cases see Adrienne Stone, 'The Limits of Constitutional Text and Structure: Standards of Review and the Freedom of Political Communication', 23 *Melbourne University Law Review* (1999) 668.

52 *Leeth v Commonwealth* (1992) 174 CLR 455.

53 Murray Gleeson, *The Rule of Law and the Constitution*, p 63.

54 *Dietrich v R* (1992) 177 CLR 292.

55 Murray Gleeson, *The Rule of Law and the Constitution*, p 16.

56 Murray Gleeson, *The Rule of Law and the Constitution*, p 56.

57 *Kartinyeri v Commonwealth* (1998) 195 CLR 337.

58 Quoted in George Williams, *A Bill of Rights for Australia*, UNSW Press, Sydney, 2000, p 8.

59 Jon Faine & Michael Pearce, 'An interview with Gareth Evans: Blueprints for reform', 8 *Legal Service Bulletin* (1983) 117, p 118.

60 See Chapter 3.

61 Except in relation to Division 4 of the Act, which extends ILO Convention 111 on Discrimination in Respect of Employment and Occupation to the States and Territories.

62 HREOC Act 1986 (Cth), section 11 (e).

63 For example, HREOC Act 1986 (Cth), section 11 (g), (h), (j), (n).

64 HREOC Act 1986 (Cth), section 11 (1) (o).

65 Human Rights Legislation Amendment Bill (no 2) 1998 (Cth).

66 HREOC, *Bringing Them Home*, AGPS, Canberra, 1997.

67 Robert McClelland, 'A charter of rights and aspirations: relevance to modern Australia', 15 November 2000, available at www.onlineopinion.com.au.

68 Constitutional Amendment (Post-War Reconstruction and Democratic Rights) Bill 1944 (Cth).

69 Constitutional Commission, *First Report of the Constitutional Commission*, AGPS, Canberra, 1988.

70 Constitutional Alteration (Rights and Freedoms) Bill 1988 (Cth).

71 Gary W Gallagher & Alan T Nolan, *The Myth of the Lost Cause and Civil War History*, Indiana University Press, Bloomington, 2000.

72 Owen Dixon, 'Two Constitutions Compared' in *Jesting Pilate and Other Papers and Addresses Collected by Judge Woinarski*, Law Book Company, Melbourne, 1965, 100, p 102.

73 Robert Menzies, *Central Power in the Australian Commonwealth*, Cassel, London, 1967, p 54.

74 Bob Carr, 'Only people — not bills — protect rights', *The Australian*, 9 January 2001, p 17.

75 Attorney-General, News Release, 13 May 2001.

76 John Howard, 'Democracy built on a fair-go ethic', *The Australian*, 10 May 2001, p 11.

77 Ian Marsh, *Institutions on the Edge? Capacity for Governance*, Allen & Unwin, Sydney, 2000.

78 Hugh Collins, 'Political Ideology in Australia: The Distinctiveness of a Benthamite Society', *Daedalus*, 1985 147.

79 Jeremy Bentham, 'Anarchical Fallacies' and 'Leading Principles of a Constitutional Code for Any State', both reprinted in J Bowring (ed), *The Works of Jeremy Bentham*, W Tait, Edinburgh, 1843, at 489 and 269 respectively.

80 Martha Nussbaum, *Women and Human Development*, Cambridge University Press, Cambridge, 2000, p 62.

81 Laurence Tribe, *American Constitutional Law*, Foundation Press, New York, 1978, p 10.

82 Jeremy Webber, 'Constitutional reticence', 25 *Australian Journal of Legal Philosophy* (2000) 125.

83 Geoffrey Sawer, *Australian Federalism in the Courts*, Melbourne University Press, Melbourne, 1967, p 208.

CHAPTER 2 THE INTERNATIONAL HUMAN RIGHTS SYSTEM

1   Johan Galtung, *Human Rights in Another Key*, Polity Press, Oxford, 1994, p 2.

2   Roberto Unger, quoted in Harvard Law School Human Rights Program, *Economic and Social Rights and the Right to Health*, Harvard Law School, Cambridge, 1995, p 13.

3   Roberto Unger, quoted in Harvard Law School Human Rights Program, *Economic and Social Rights and the Right to Health*, Harvard Law School, Cambridge, 1995, p 13.

4   See Immanuel Kant, *The Metaphysics of Morals*, Cambridge University Press, Cambridge, 1996, pp 186–87.

5   Ronald Dworkin, *Taking Rights Seriously*, Duckworth, London,1977, p xi.

6   Ronald Dworkin, *Taking Rights Seriously*, pp 198–99.

7   Ronald Dworkin, *Taking Rights Seriously*, p 204.

8   *Sophocles' Antigone* (Andrew Brown (ed), Aris & Phillips, Warminster,1987) p 59, lines 450–70.

9   Kim Dae-Jung, 'Embrace the best of East and West to shape a better world', *The Australian*, 3 September 1996, p 13.

10 Alfred Scheepers, *A Survey of Buddhist Thought*, Olive Press, Amsterdam,1994, pp 122–26.

11 Gopinath Dhawan, *The Political Philosophy of Mahatma Gandhi*, Navajiran, Ahmenabad,1946, chapters II and III.

12 See the Final Act of the International Conference on Human Rights held in Teheran in 1968 (UN Doc. A/CONF. 32/41 at 3 UN Publ. E. 68 XIV 2) and the Declaration of the Second World Conference on Human Rights held in Vienna in 1993 (UN Doc. A/CONF.157/24).

13 See *Advisory Opinion on Namibia* (1971) ICJ Rep. 16, p 57.

14 'Great divide on human rights', *The Australian*, 30 August 1997, p 1.

15 Yash Ghai, 'Human Rights and Governance: The Asia Debate', 10 *Australian Year Book of International Law* (1994) 1.

16 'Media and Society in Asia', speech at the Asian Press Forum, Hong Kong, 2 December 1994.

17 Makau Mutua, 'Savages, Victims, and Saviors: The Metaphor of Human Rights', 42 *Harvard International Law Journal* (2001) 201.

18 Maurice Cranston, 'Are there any human rights?', *Daedalus* (Fall 1983), 255.

19 ICCPR, article 2 (3) (a).

20 ICESCR, article 2 (1).

21 Craig Scott, 'The interdependence and permeability of human rights norms: towards a partial fusion of the International Covenants on Human Rights', 27 *Osgoode Hall Law Journal* (1989) 769.

22 Department of Foreign Affairs and Trade, *Human Rights Manual* (2nd ed, 1998) pp 13–14.

23 Allyson M Pollock & David Price, 'Rewriting the regulations: how the World Trade Organisation could accelerate privatisation in health care systems' 356 *The Lancet* 2000 (1995).

24 Roberto Unger, *False Necessity*, Cambridge University Press, Cambridge, 1987, pp 508–510.

25 Costas Douzinas, *The End of Human Rights*, Hart Publishing, Cambridge, 2000, p 7.

26 For example, Andrea Wolper & Julie Peters (eds), *Women's Rights, Human Rights*, Routledge, New York, 1995.

27 Martha Minow, 'Interpreting rights: an essay for Robert Cover', 96 *Yale Law Journal* (1987) 1860, p 1910.

28 Albie Sachs, quoted in *Economic and Social Rights and the Right to Health*, p 42.

29 John Humphrey, *Human Rights and the United Nations: A Great Adventure*, Transnational Publishers, New York, 1984, p 67.

30 For example, ICCPR, articles 18 and 26.

31 John Humphrey, *Human Rights and the United Nations*, p 68.

32 See John Witte, 'Law, Religion, and Human Rights', 28 *Columbia Human Rights Law Review* (1996) 1, p 9.

33 See Max Charlesworth, *Religious Inventions*, Cambridge University Press, Cambridge, 1997, pp 120–22.

34 John Witte, 'Law, Religion, and Human Rights', pp 10–11.

35 Section 37 (a).

36 Section 37 (d).

37 'Churches angered by attack on rights', *The Australian*, 30 October 2000, p 5.

38 John Witte, 'Law, Religion, and Human Rights', pp 15–16.

39 Abdullahi An-Na'im, 'Human Rights in the Muslim World: Socio-Political Conditions and Scriptural Imperatives', 3 *Harvard Human Rights Journal* (1990) 13, pp 46–47.

40 See, for example, Elizabeth Schussler Fiorenza, *In Memory of Her: A Feminist Theological Reconstruction of Christian Origins*, Crossroad, New York, 1983.

41 Arati Rao, 'The Politics of Gender and Culture in International Human Rights Discourse' in Andrea Wolper & Julie Peters (eds), *Women's Rights, Human Rights*, 167, p 174.

42 Peter Van Ness, 'Introduction: In Search of Common Ground' in Peter Van Ness (ed), *Debating Human Rights: Critical Essays from the United States and Asia*, Routledge, London, 1999, 1, p 17.

CHAPTER 3 PROTECTING HUMAN RIGHTS IN AUSTRALIA

1 Australian Constitution, section 51 (xxix).

2 See the Committee's Concluding Observations, UN Doc. CERD/C/304/Add 101, 19 April 2000.

3 Sex Discrimination Act (Cth), section 40.

4 Sex Discrimination Act (Cth), sections 36, 37, 38, 39 and 42.

5 Sex Discrimination Act (Cth), section 41.

6 Sex Discrimination Act (Cth), section 43.

7 Sex Discrimination Amendment Bill (no 1) 2000.

8 For example, UN Doc. CCPR/C/SR 1856, 1858, 27, 28 July 2000; CCPR/CO/69/AUS, 28 July 2000; E/C.12/1/Add.50, 1 September 2000.

9 (1992) 175 CLR 1, 42.

10 *Minister for Immigration and Ethnic Affairs v Teoh* (1995) 183 CLR 273.

11 Statement of 10 May 1995, reprinted in 17 *Australian Year Book of International Law* (1996) 552–53.

12 Statement of 25 February 1997, reprinted in 19 *Australian Year Book of International Law* (1998) 224.

13 For example, Administrative Decisions (Effect of International Instruments) Bill 1999.

14 For example, *Jago v District Court of New South Wales* (1988) 12 NSWLR 558.

15 *Kartinyeri v Commonwealth* (1998) 195 CLR 337, 416.

16 Amelia Simpson and George Williams, 'International Law and Constitutional Interpretation', 11 *Public Law Review* (2000) 205.

17 (1999) 165 ALR 621.

18 *International Tin Council Case* [1990] 2 AC 418; Ian Brownlie, *Principles of Public International Law*, 5th ed, Clarendon Press, Oxford, 1998, p 42.

19 Optional Protocol to the ICCPR.

20 Article 14.

21 Article 22.

22 Australia also accepted the right of other state parties to these treaties to complain about Australian breaches of the treaty commitments (ICCPR article 40, CERD article 11, CAT article 21). This procedure has not yet been used.

23 ICCPR Communication 488/1992.

24 ICCPR Communication 560/1993.

25 CAT Communication 120/1998.

26 *Canberra Times*, 19 February 2000, p 1.

27 Joint media release A 97, 29 August 2000 available at www.dfat.gov.au/media/releases/foreign/2000.

28 See Ann Kent, *China, the United Nations, and Human Rights*, University of Pennsylvania Press, Philadelphia, 1999, pp 155–60.

29 See Henry J Steiner and Philip Alston, *International Human Rights in Context*, 2nd ed, Oxford University Press, Oxford, 2000, pp 1029–1042.

30 'PM rejects Fraser's call for rights bill', *Canberra Times*, 26 August 2000, p 3.

31 *R v Drybones* 1970 SCR 282.

32 *Robertson and Rosetanni v R* 1963 SCR 651.

33 *Attorney-General v Lavell* 1974 SCR 1349.

34 Section 1.

35 Section 33.

36 *Andrews v Law Society of British Columbia* [1989] 1 SCR 143.

37 Joel Bakan, *Just Words: Constitutional Rights and Social Wrongs*, University of Toronto Press, Toronto, 1997, chapter 5.

38 *R v Big M Drug Mart* [1985] 1 SCR 295.

39 R v *Zundel* [1992] 2 SCR 731.

40 Section 36.

41 Section 8.

42 *The National Coalition for Gay and Lesbian Equality and others v Minister for Home Affairs*, 3 BCLR 280 (1999), reprinted in 39 *International Legal Materials* (2000) 798.

43 6 BCLR (1995) 665.

44 12 BCLR (1997) 1696.

45 Case 11/00, judgment available at www.law.wits.ac.za/court.

46 The Act came into operation in Scotland in 1999 under the scheme of devolution.

47   Sections 3(1) and 3 (2) (a).
48   Section 2.
49   Section 4.
50   Section 6.
51   Section 6 (3).
52   Keith Ewing, 'The Human Rights Act and Parliamentary Democracy' 62 *Modern Law Review* (1999) 79.
53   Section 10 gives special powers to 'fast track' legislative amendments after a Declaration of Incompatibility is made.
54   Francesca Klug, 'The Human Rights Act: A Third Way or a Third Wave Bill of Rights?', speech given at Kings College, London on 27 March 2001, available at http://www.kcl.ac.uk/depsta/law/research/hraru/research/.
55   Article 6(1).
56   *Starrs v Ruxton* [2000] SLT 42.
57   Article 5.
58   *R (H) v Mental Health Tribunal North and East London Region* (unreported 28 March 2001)
59   Available at www.homeoffice.gov.uk/hract/guidance.htm.
60   Australian Law Reform Commission, *Equality Before the Law*, AGPS, Canberra, 1994.
61   Frank Brennan, *Legislating Liberty: A Bill of Rights for Australia*, Queensland University Press, Brisbane, 1998.
62   Brian Galligan and Ian McAllister, 'Citizen and elite attitudes towards an Australian Bill of Rights', in Charles Sampford (ed), *Rethinking Human Rights*, Federation Press, Sydney, 1997, 144.
63   Mark Tushnet, *Taking the Constitution away from the Courts*, Princeton University Press, Princeton, 1999.
64   Mark Tushnet, *Taking the Constitution away from the Courts*, Chapter 3.
65   The Australian Democrats' Australian Bill of Rights Bill 2000 (available at http://www.democrats.org.au/campaigns/billrights/) takes this approach: section 8 (2).
66   Janet Hiebert, 'Why must a Bill of Rights be a contest of political wills? The Canadian alternative', 10 *Public Law Review* (1999) 22.
67   George Williams, *A Bill of Rights for Australia*, UNSW Press, Sydney, p 49.
68   10 BCLR (1996) 1253.
69   10 BCLR (1996) 1253, paragraph 78.
70   For example, Universal Declaration of Human Rights, article 29.
71   For a discussion of this point in the United Kingdom context see Francesca Klug 'The Human Rights Act: A Third Way or a Third Wave Bill of Rights?'.
72   Bertolt Brecht, *Poems 1913–1956* (John Willett and Ralph Manheim (eds)) Methuen, New York, 1976, p 400.